sixty mi

GO

around London

BARRIE & JENKINS
COMMUNICA - EUROPA

First Published 1975 by
Barrie & Jenkins Ltd
24 Highbury Crescent
London N5 1RX

Typeset by Finsbury Park Typesetters Ltd, London
Printed and bound in Great Britain by
Redwood Burn Limited, Trowbridge & Esher

EDITOR'S FOREWORD

When I lived in London I was lucky enough to be near two of its finest open spaces, and as I walked across Hampstead Heath or strolled through Regent's Park I often thought to myself how fortunate Londoners were to have so many magnificent open spaces.

Naturally there are no golf courses quite as near St Paul's or Trafalgar Square as Regent's Park, but Hampstead or Highgate to the north, and Dulwich to the south are not much further away than the extremities of the famous Heath. And it doesn't take long, by tube or train, to get to clubs such as Wanstead, Ealing, Wimbledon Park or Royal Mid-Surrey. I take these just as examples, for there are many other clubs within equally easy reach of the centre of London.

I have come to the conclusion that cars are a liability in the capital, because of the inevitable traffic jams which endure for most of the day and especially during the morning and evening rush hours. I publicise this aspect of London travel because in many cases it could be quicker and more comfortable to go by train. Some golf courses, such as Sunningdale, are only a few minutes' walk from the station, but if there is a distance to go one can usually find a taxi at most stations in London's suburbs and surrounding country.

There are two categories of golfers who would like to play on courses in and around London: those who live in the metropolis or its environs, and those who come as visitors, many from overseas. The former naturally wish to play on a course fairly near their home or within a reasonable distance; the latter, as a rule, want to play on famous courses that they have heard or read about, or seen on television. They may wish to stay in London and travel out, or they may prefer to stay at a hotel, say in the Ascot or Wentworth area, and make that their base.

In such a large area as is covered in this book there is a wide variety of courses, ranging from humble affairs which exist on some of London's commons to the lush Wentworths and Walton Heaths. Did you know, by the way, that there is a golf course in the centre of the famous Ascot racecourse? And did you know that the headquarters of the Moor Park Club is one of the most historic houses in Britain? Did you know that on the edge of Wimbledon Common, the home of the London Scottish Club, the oldest club in England to be playing on its original course, there is a beautiful windmill? So apart from the opportunity to play on a great variety of courses, there are some interesting facts to discover and much natural beauty to enjoy.

All the Home Counties have many splendid golf courses, but although I myself now live in Buckinghamshire, which is not short of good courses, I have to admit that Surrey is the luckiest in respect of its golfing terrain. Much of Surrey, indeed most, is on sand and gravel and so the whole of the county can be described as ideal golf country. I could reel off the names of dozens of Surrey courses, all with the same sandy characteristics. And where there is sand you also get heathland and pine trees. For many enthusiasts such qualities are essentials for a good golf course. I would not go as far as to say that, but certainly sand, heather, gorse and pine trees go to make for good golf in attractive surroundings. Woking, West Hill, Camberley, Addington, Walton Heath and Wentworth are good examples of what I mean. Sunningdale, I always feel, should be included in the Surrey courses but in fact it is just across the border in Berkshire.

Heath courses are also to be found in Sussex and in Hampshire—North Hants is a magnificent course of this type—but further from London, to the south, the country changes, and towards the coast becomes downland. To the west there are fine courses such as Stoke Poges, and further north Denham, Ashridge, Moor Park; these are mainly parkland, some of them having just a little heathland. Courses in Middlesex, Hertfordshire and Bedfordshire, and in counties further north, are also mostly parkland, but in the east, Essex has a mixture of courses of all kinds. Kent has an even greater variety, with seaside links as well.

Golfers based in London and its environs may be at a disadvantage, by comparison with those who live in rural districts, because they may have to go further for their golf, but the travel is worthwhile. Generally speaking, the further out of London you go the better the chances of getting a quiet game. But wherever you choose, I would make one recommendation: try to contact the club in advance. You might make the journey there and then discover that a big Society meeting is on, and the course is closed to visitors for the day. So telephone first to avoid being disappointed.

Most golf courses, though not all, will usually welcome visitors on payment of the appropriate green fee. It is better, if possible, to take with you an introduction from the Secretary of your home club. This acts as a reference, and many golf clubs quite rightly like to know who is using their course and premises. There is one rather dismal point I should mention. At the time I write most golf clubs are full up and cannot take any new members. The situation may change, however, in the not too distant future: some people, at present members of two clubs, may decide to give up one, and other people, perhaps getting on a bit, may decide that the ever-increasing subscriptions are becoming too much for them. Golf clubs will need to take more members if they are to survive. The fact is that, except for Society meetings, many golf clubs these days are empty during the week. That situation cannot endure and it will mean, eventually, that more new members will have to be admitted.

This present volume is the successor to *Fifty Miles of Golf Round London.* Its scope is considerably wider, and its contents are up to date at the time of going to press. This could not have been achieved without the kind co-operation of the Secretaries of all the clubs mentioned, to whom I tender my grateful thanks.

GOLF COURSE DESIGN
The constant challenge

J. Hamilton Stutt
Vice Chairman, British Association of Golf Course Architects

Early paintings show that a form of golf on ice must have been fairly popular in Holland as far back as the Middle Ages, but there is little doubt that golf as we know it originated on the seaside sand dunes of Scotland.

Golfers would play along until they saw, perhaps, a little patch of smooth grass nestling in among the sand dunes, just inviting a shot. These became the first greens. After holing out, perhaps in a convenient rabbit scrape, some sand would be taken out of the hole and this used to tee up (within two club lengths) for the next shot.

It is probably not widely known that the game of golf is 18 holes purely by chance. The good people of St Andrews started with 22 holes but finally settled on 9 of these natural green sites, among the sand dunes, on the way 'out'. Coming back home towards 'the auld grey toon' they played into exactly the same holes, with an extra home hole beside the first tee, nice and handy for the nearest hostelry. Voilà, 18 holes! It was not until much later, in 1832, that separate holes were cut for the inward half, so giving the famous double greens.

Although there would be no clearly defined fairways as we know them today, many players' second or third shots on these early links courses tended to be played from the same areas. These must soon have become worn down to the bare sand. Further wear and natural erosion deepened and enlarged these patches into what we now call bunkers, all of them, by virtue of their formation, being automatically located in the most diabolically awkward places. The existence of a majority of these natural bunkers on the right hand side confirms that slicing is not a malady afflicting modern golfers only.

Only twice in nearly thirty years, once in Britain and once in Spain, have I had the sheer delight of planning golf holes among natural sand dunes in exactly the same manner as our ancestors of over five hundred years ago. On every other kind of ground the golf course has to be created by the architect. Some sites, of course, are much better than others, but each has its own particular problems—or challenges as I like to think of them—which the golf architect, using all his skill and experience, must try to overcome. Very little has been written on this subject, probably because the few really experienced golf course architects in the world are such busy men, but at least the main requirements to be satisfied in designing a golf course may be summarised under the following headings.

Making the best use of natural features With very few exceptions a chosen site will have at least one desirable feature, perhaps some attractive natural green sites, fine existing trees, a pond or even a fine view. Construction costs are greatly reduced by the maximum use of natural features, and of course the finished course is much better.

To make the most of a site in this way does require great care, an intimate knowledge of the ground, and much more time for planning. Too many golf courses, in the past, have been designed in a rush, or allegedly completed in airport waiting rooms! Sometimes I will take several weeks over the initial layout plan, to make sure that the best possible layout has been achieved for the ground, with nothing missed, and to try to avoid expensive changes being needed later, to put right something which should have been thought of beforehand.

Pleasure for all types of golfer This, after all, is the object of the whole exercise. Golfers are human, and even the 24 handicap man likes to feel he is playing on a first-class golf course which can also test the experts. This is best done by the skilful placing of hazards to make the expert *think,* and at the same time give just and worthwhile reward for any golfers capable of long and accurate hitting. Too often golf design encourages a negative approach and safety play, e.g. irons off the tee. I will have none of this 'pussy' golf! At the same time, except in special circumstances, I am agin the very long golf course where the length is purely a status symbol. Such courses are a misery to most golfers, besides being extravagant in land, and expensive to construct and maintain.

The expert, it must be remembered, only gets his golf at all by courtesy of medium or high handicap players and beginners, who represent perhaps 95% of all golfers. The influence of low handicap players in an average golf club is out of all proportion to their numbers, and the architect must try to keep a better balance and cater for all grades of player. This is particularly important nowadays, with large numbers of complete beginners coming in to golf. I try to cater for the average golfer in the following ways:

(a) Avoidance of deep rough and other potential lost ball areas within 10-15 yards of fairways, etc. Today's golf courses being so crowded, the frustrating, time-consuming business of looking for lost balls should be eliminated altogether. By having zones of semi-rough where players may lose a stroke, but not a ball, fairways can be narrowed and shaped better, so that golf can also be a fairer and more interesting test for all.

(b) Ample level areas on greens to reduce the chances of 3 putting, so disheartening to us all, as any visit to a locker room after a competition will confirm.

The excessive slopes popular with some architects, particularly overseas, do not make for enjoyable golf. They also reduce the number of places to which the pin can be moved to combat today's heavy wear from play. I believe that a good iron shot to within, say, 9 ft of the pin should normally be rewarded by a fairly level, straight putt and the chance of a birdie. Freakishly sloping greens, like poor ones, undoubtedly tend to level down golfing skills and deny the better golfer his just advantage. Gentle slopes and features towards the perimeter of greens should, of course, be formed for appearance and to add interest to longer approach putts and pitches.

(c) A wide range of teeing positions to provide maximum variety in length and play of each hole. Really large tees also help the problem of wear. I have always believed in large tees, but, acting on experience, I am now increasing tee sizes even further. The wear being caused by the increased proportion of beginners on new courses has to be seen to be believed. Fortunately, with the new Triplex mowers, the mowing of large tee areas is no longer a problem.

Quart into a pint pot Land prices being what they are, it is very seldom that one ever has as much land for a new golf course as one would like. One must try, therefore, to strike the best compromise between adequate length and such conflicting requirements as well-spaced fairways, best use of attractive features, varied length and orientation of holes, retention of fine trees, etc. Once again, a skilled initial layout plan is all-important.

Space must also be found near the club house for a good practice ground (which I regard as essential), for putting greens, and really adequate car parking. The modern Country Club must also have space for squash, tennis, a swimming pool, and any other activities dreamed up by a far-seeing promoter.

Practical construction 'know-how' The complete golf architect must be an expert on golf course construction, and ideally should know as much about the subject as any contractor he is likely to be supervising, if not more. I personally regard this as most important. For example, although wonders can be done with modern earth-moving machinery, it is important to know what would be practical, and what would be hideously expensive and disruptive.

Besides being able to draw up a really detailed 'cast iron' specification and plan, suitable for competitive tendering if required, the architect must also be able to tailor this exactly to the needs of the client and of the site. Golf courses, like motor cars, can be of varying standard and vastly different cost. A 'Rolls Royce' may be all right for some, but for others a 'Jaguar' or even a 'Mini' may be equally suitable and a more viable proposition economically. I find there can often be just as much personal satisfaction in designing a new golf course for a small town community, working on a shoe string, as in a multi-million-dollar project overseas. It is the people who count.

To most golfers a golf course is only as good as the turf and soil it is played on. Knowledge of drainage, grass seeds, soils and greenkeeping are life-time studies, where a little knowledge is very dangerous and about which no golf course architect can ever know too much. Although expert advice can be obtained on these subjects, it is very much better if the architect is himself an expert. Decisions have to be made constantly throughout planning, specifying and construction.

Beauty It is no use coping with all the challenges described above if the finished golf course does not possess that indefinable quality of natural beauty.

A well-designed golf course should enhance its surroundings, yet blend completely with them. The golf architect knows he has been successful if the finished golf course looks as if it had always been there, and draws the comment 'How lucky you were to have all those features there already'.

I must confess to being very fortunate, for I can now choose to plan new golf courses only on sites or in areas which appeal to me. Occasionally, however, the challenge overcomes one's better judgement, as with my new course on a rocky barren hillside outside Beirut (the only site then available), and my other course at present being constructed on a derelict slag heap in Northumberland. There is a special satisfaction in trying to overcome these natural disadvantages and create something of lasting use and beauty out of ugliness.

Perhaps this is why nearly every golfer would like to be a golf course architect.

DRIVING RANGES

CHATHAM Chatham Golf Centre Ltd, Street End Road, Chatham, Kent (tel: Medway 48925, 48907)

COBHAM Fairmile Golf Range, Portsmouth Road, Cobham, Surrey (tel: Cobham 4419)

COLNBROOK Gallymead Golf Driving Range, Old Bath Road, Colnbrook, Bucks. (tel: Colnbrook 2772)

CRAWLEY Fairway Golf Driving Range, Horsham Road, Pease Pottage, Crawley, Sussex (tel: Crawley 33000)

CROYDON Croydon Driving Range, 175 Long Lane, Croydon, Surrey (tel: 654 7859)

EALING Ealing Golf Range, Rowdell Road, Northolt, Middx. (tel: Viking 4967)

ESHER John Jacobs Golf Centre, Sandown Park, More Lane, Esher, Surrey (tel: Esher 63340)

FETCHAM Riverside Club and Golf Driving Range, River Lane, Fetcham, Nr. Leatherhead, Surrey (tel: Leatherhead 5713)

GREENFORD Greenford Golf Centre, Rockware Avenue, Greenford Road, Greenford, Middx. (tel: 01-548 3949)

HASTINGS Driving Ranges Ltd, Bulverhythe Recreation Ground, St Leonards-on-Sea, Hastings, Sussex

LONDON Peter Butler Golf Dome, Scrubs Lane, London W.12 (tel: 01-749 1418) Golf Centres Ltd, 444 High Road, Finchley, London N.12 (tel: 01-445 0411)

RICHMOND Golf Driving Range, Athletic Ground, Chertsey Road, Surrey (tel: Richmond 0397)

SURBITON Surbiton Golf Range, Woodstock Lane, Chessington, Surrey (tel: Emberbrook 2618)

WALTON-ON-THAMES Walton Driving Range, The Towpath, Walton-on-Thames, Surrey (tel: Walton-on-Thames 27659)

WATFORD Watford Golf Driving Range, Sheepcot Lane, North Orbital Road, Garston, Watford, Herts. (tel: Garston 75560)

WELWYN GARDEN CITY Welwyn Golf Driving Range, Gosling Stadium, Stanborough Road, Welwyn Garden City, Herts. (tel: Welwyn Garden 20017)

NOTES

VAT

The Editor would like to point out that figures given for subscriptions, entrance fees and green fees will be subject to change, according to variations in VAT since the time of going to press. Please ask the club secretary for confirmation.

Introductions

An introduction is not needed at a Municipal golf course. At a private club an introduction is always advisable, but only when it is essential is it mentioned in the entries.

Membership

If details are not given in the entry, please apply to the club secretary.

ABRIDGE (1)

Stapleford Tawney, Essex RM4 1ST

Tel: Stapleford 396

Founded 1964 340 members Venue for the 1971 Martini International Tournament

18 holes 6,543 yards S.S.S. 71

Green fees Mon.-Fri. £2.50 per rd. £3.50 per day
Weekends with member only
Introduction necessary

Visiting societies Max. 40 Terms by arrangement

Meals Bar snacks only

Nearest railway station Debden (Central line tube)

Hotels in vicinity Bell Motel, Epping

ADDINGTON (2)

Shirley Church Road, Croydon, Surrey

Tel: 01-777 1055

Founded 1913

18 holes 6,216 yards S.S.S. 70 Parkland

Green fees Mon.-Fri. £1.75
Weekends £3
Visitors must be introduced by members at weekends

Visiting societies Terms by arrangement

Nearest railway station East Croydon 2½ miles

Hotels in vicinity Selsdon Park, Sanderstead; Elgin Court, Croydon

ADDINGTON COURT (3)

Featherbed Lane, Addington, Croydon, Surrey CRO 9AA

Tel: 01-657 0281

Founded 1932 54 holes public course

Green fees	**Old (18)**	**New (18)**	**Lower (9)**
	5,710 yds	5,515 yds	2,305 yds (x2)
Mon.-Fri.	60p	49p	27p
Weekends	82p	66p	44p

Visitors advised to book one week in advance for weekend play on Old and New courses

Professional

Membership Strictly limited, lists currently closed

Visiting societies Max. 24 Weekdays only

Meals Lunch, tea and snacks
Nearest railway station East Croydon $2\frac{1}{2}$ miles
Hotels in vicinity Selsdon Park, Sanderstead

ADDINGTON PALACE (4)

Addington Park, Gravel Hill, Croydon, Surrey
Tel: 01-654 3061

Founded 1930 500 members
18 holes 6,410 yards S.S.S. 71
Green fees Mon.-Fri. £2.50
Introduction necessary
Professional M. Pilkington
Membership Full subscription £60 p.a. (E.F. £60)
Visiting Societies £5 per head
Meals Available Tues. to Fri. inc.
Nearest railway station East Croydon
Hotels in vicinity Elgin, Croydon; Farmhouse Restaurant, Croydon

ALDERSHOT COMMAND (5)

Laffan's Road, Aldershot, Hants.
Tel: Farnborough 41104

18 holes 6,363 yards S.S.S. 70 Heath and parkland
Green fees Mon.-Fri. £2.50
Sat. £3
Sun. no visitors
Visiting societies By arrangement
Meals Full restaurant facility
Nearest railway station Guildford
Hotels in vicinity Queen's, Farnborough

ALRESFORD (6)

Cherston Road, Alresford, Hants.
Tel: Alresford 3153/3746

Founded 1903
9 holes 5,901 yards S.S.S. 68 Undulating and wooded
Green fees Mon.-Fri. £1
Weekends £2
Public holidays £2

Professional W. Young
Membership Lists closed
Visiting societies Not normally accepted
Meals Not available
Nearest railway station Winchester 7 miles
Hotels in vicinity Bell and Swan, Alresford

ALTON (7)

Old Odiham Road, Alton, Hants.
Tel: Alton 82042

Founded 1908
9 holes 5,592 yards S.S.S. 67 Hilly
Green fees Mon.-Fri. £1 per rd.
Weekends £2
Public holidays £2
Professional P. Stanwick
Membership Lists closed
Visiting societies By arrangement
Meals Not available
Nearest railway station Alton approx. 2 miles
Hotels in vicinity Swan, Alton

ANDOVER (8)

51 Winchester Road, Andover, Hants.
Tel: Andover 3980

Founded 1907 340 members
9 holes 5,630 yards S.S.S. 67 Hilly downland
Green fees Mon.-Fri. 75p per rd.
Weekends £1.60 per rd.
Introduction necessary
No visitors before midday on Sun.
Professional J. Woodman
Membership Full subscription £7.70 p.a. (E.F. £3.50)
Visiting Societies No provision
Meals Not available
Nearest railway station Andover 4 miles
Hotels in vicinity Star & Garter and White Hart, Andover

ARKLEY (9)

Rowley Green Road, Barnet, Herts. EN5 3HL

Tel: 01-449 0394

Founded 1909 400 members

9 holes 6,014 yards S.S.S. 69 (18 tees) Wooded and undulating

Green fees Mon.-Fri. £2 per rd. £3 per day
Weekends with member only

Professional R. Gerken

Membership Full subscription £33 p.a. (E.F. £25)

Visiting societies £2.50 per head Meals by arrangement

Meals Lunch and snacks every day

Nearest railway station High Barnet 2 miles

Hotels in vicinity Hadley, Barnet

ASCOT HEATH (10)

Winkfield Road, Ascot, Berks.

Tel: Ascot 22923

Founded 1887 350 members
Venue of first British Boys' Championship, 1920

18 holes 5,530 yards S.S.S. 67 Heathland course in centre of Ascot Racecourse

Green fees Mon.-Fri. only £1.35 per rd.
No introduction necessary
No golf on race days

Professional A. C. J. Haylett

Visiting societies Not catered for

Meals Light refreshments only

Nearest railway station Ascot 1 mile

Hotels in vicinity Berystede, Royal Berkshire, and Royal Foresters, Ascot

ASHFORD (11)

Sandyhurst Lane, Ashford, Kent TN25 4NT

Tel: Ashford 20180

18 holes 6,442 yards S.S.S. 71 Parkland

Green fees Mon.-Fri. £1.30 per rd.
Weekends £2.25
Not before 11 a.m. on Sun. unless with a member

Visiting societies Terms by arrangement

Meals Bar snacks always available
Other meals, 24 hours' notice requested

Nearest railway station Ashford $1\frac{1}{2}$ miles

Hotel in vicinity George, Ashford

ASHRIDGE (12)

The Clubhouse, Little Gaddesden, Nr Berkhamsted, Herts.

Tel: Little Gaddesden 2244

Founded 1932

18 holes 6,508 yards S.S.S. 71 Parkland

Green fees Mon.-Fri. £2.20 per rd. £3.30 per day
By prior arrangement with the Secretary

Professional Alex Hay

Membership Full subscription £50 p.a. (E.F. £90)
Waiting list

Visiting societies £5.50 per head, fully inc.

Meals Lunch and tea (to be booked prior to play)

Nearest railway station Berkhamsted 5 miles

Hotels in vicinity Bell, Aston Clinton; Bridgewater Arms, Little Gaddesden

ASPLEY GUISE & WOBURN SANDS (13)

West Hill, Aspley Guise, Milton Keynes, Beds.

Tel: Woburn Sands 2264

Founded 1914 500 members

18 holes 6,200 yards Undulating course, mostly sandy

Green fees £2 per rd. £3 per day
50p reduction with member

Professional Les Wright

Membership Full subscription £35 p.a. (E.F. £50)

Visiting societies Max. 40 Wed. & Fri. only. Fees by arrangement

Meals Available

Nearest railway station Woburn Sands 1 mile

Hotels in vicinity Swan, Woburn Sands; Bell, Aspley Guise

BANSTEAD DOWNS (14)

Burdon Lane, Belmont, Sutton, Surrey

Tel: 01-642 2284

Founded 1890 650 members

18 holes 6,190 yards S.S.S. 69 Downland

Green fees Mon.-Fri. £2 per day (£1.50 after 12 noon)
Introduction necessary

Professional I. Marr

Visiting societies Confined to introduction by member

Meals Available (except Mon.)

Nearest railway station Belmont

Hotels in vicinity Drift Bridge, Epsom

BARNEHURST (15)

Mayplace Road, Barnehurst, Bexleyheath, Kent

Tel: Crayford 23746

9 holes 5,146 yards S.S.S. 66 Parkland

Green fees On application to the Secretary

Professional J. Thomson

Visiting societies Not catered for
Bona fide club members welcome at all times

Nearest railway station Bexleyheath

Hotels in vicinity Royal Victoria & Bull, Dartford

BASILDON (16)

Kingswood, Basildon, Essex

Tel: Basildon 3760

18 holes 6,083 yards S.S.S. 70 Parkland

Green fees Mon.-Fri. 50p
Weekends £1.20
Public course, no introduction necessary

Membership Private club playing over course
Nominal membership plus course season ticket

Visiting societies By arrangement

Meals Lunch available every day

Nearest railway station Basildon

Hotels in vicinity Essex Centre, Basildon

BASINGSTOKE (17)

Kempshott Park, Basingstoke, Hants.

Tel: Basingstoke 65990

Founded 1926 650 members Birthplace of Miss Molly Gourlay; course made from her private 9-holes course

18 holes 6,280 yards Old Deer Park, undulating and very picturesque

Green fees Mon.-Fri. £1.25 per rd.
Weekends with member only
Bona fide club members only

Professional Stan Hills

Membership Full subscription £30 p.a. (E.F. £25)

Visiting societies Max. 40 £4.40 per head

Meals Every day (except Mon.)

Nearest railway station Basingstoke 4 miles

Hotels in vicinity Golden Lion and Red Lion, Basingstoke

BATCHWOOD HALL (18)

Batchwood Drive, St Albans, Herts.

Tel: St Albans 54756

Founded 1936 250 members Playing over Batchwood Hall Municipal Golf Course

18 holes 6,544 yards S.S.S. 71 Parkland

Green fees Mon.-Fri. 80p
Weekends £1.60

Professional A. P. Wynne

Membership Nominal subscription plus season ticket from District Council (St Albans residents only)

Visiting societies By arrangement with St Albans D.C.

Meals Minimal catering available

Nearest railway station St Albans City 2 miles

Hotels in vicinity Peahen and Noke, St Albans

BEACONSFIELD (19)

Seer Green, Beaconsfield, Bucks.

Tel: Beaconsfield 6545

Founded 1914 650 members

18 holes 6,410 yards S.S.S. 71 Parkland and woods

Green fees Mon.-Fri. £3.30 (88p with member)
Weekends £1.10 (with member only)
Must have letter of introduction

Professional Alex Crombie

Membership Full subscription £66 p.a. (E.F. £75)

Visiting societies Tues. & Wed. only £5.80 inc. meals and grats.

Meals Lunch, tea and snacks every day

Nearest railway station Seer Green 50 yards
Hotels in vicinity Saracen's Head and Royal White Hart, Beaconsfield

BEARSTED (20)

Bearsted, Maidstone, Kent
Tel: Maidstone 38389

18 holes 5,820 yards S.S.S. 68 Parkland with magnificent views of North Downs
Green fees Mon.-Fri. £2 per rd.
Weekends with member only
Visiting societies Weekdays only Terms by arrangement
Meals Bar snacks always available
Prior notice required for lunch or dinner
Nearest railway station Bearsted (adjacent)
Hotels in vicinity Park Gate, Leeds; Great Danes, Hollingbourne

BECKENHAM PLACE PARK (21)

Beckenham Place Park, Beckenham, Kent
Tel: 01-650 0812

18 holes 5,672 yards S.S.S. 67 Parkland
Green fees Mon.-Fri. 52p
Weekends 82p
Municipal course, no introduction necessary
Professional G. A. Cotton
Visiting societies Not catered for
Meals Bar snacks available
Nearest railway station Beckenham Junction ¾ mile
Beckenham Hill ¾ mile
Hotels in vicinity Bromley Court, Bromley Hill

BEDFORD & COUNTY (22)

Green Lane, Clapham, Beds. MK41 6ET
Tel: Bedford 52617

Founded 1912 550 members Venue for several county events
18 holes 6,290 yards S.S.S. 70 Undulating parkland
Green fees Mon.-Fri. £1.35 per rd. £2.15 per day
Weekends £2.45 (£1.20 per member)

Professional K. T. Warren

Membership Full subscription £40.20 p.a. (E.F. £44 inc. VAT)

Visiting societies Max. 108 £3.50 upwards per head inc. meals

Meals A la carte daily

Nearest railway station Bedford 3 miles

Hotels in vicinity Woodlands Manor, Clapham; Kimbolton, Bedford

BEDFORDSHIRE (23)

Biddenham, Bedford

Tel: Bedford 61669

18 holes 6,173 yards S.S.S. 69 Parkland

Green fees Mon.-Fri. £1.50 per rd. £2.50 per day
Weekends £3 per rd. £4 per day
Introduction necessary

Professional D. Roberts

Visiting societies Weekdays only Terms on application

Meals Lunch every day

Hotels in vicinity Swan, Bedford

BELFAIRS (24)

Eastwood Road, Leigh-on-Sea, Essex

Tel: Southend 525345

18 holes 5,890 yards S.S.S. 68 Parkland

Green fees Mon.-Fri. 60p
Weekends £1.40
Public course, no introduction necessary

Membership Private club playing over course
Nominal membership plus season ticket

Professional R. Foreman

Visiting societies By arrangement

Meals Light snacks and refreshments

Nearest railway station Leigh-on-Sea 2 miles

Hotels in vicinity Airport, Rochford

BERKHAMSTED (25)

Berkhamsted, Herts. HP4 2QD

Tel: Berkhamsted 3730

Founded 1890 600 members Venue for annual Berkhamsted Trophy

18 holes 6,545 yards S.S.S. 72 Heathland, no sand bunkers on course

Green fees Mon.-Fri. £2 per rd.
Weekends £3.50 per rd. (after 11.30 a.m. only)
Introduction essential

Professional B. J. Proudfoot

Membership Full subscription £44 p.a. (E.F. £50)

Visiting societies Max. 60 £5 per head

Meals Lunch and tea daily

Nearest railway station Berkhamsted

Hotels in vicinity Swan, Berkhamsted; Post House, Hemel Hempstead; Bridgewater Arms, Little Gaddesden

BERKSHIRE (26)

Swinley Road, Ascot, Berks.

Tel: Ascot 21495

Founded 1928

36 holes Red: 6,459 yds. S.S.S. 71
Blue: 6,351 yds. S.S.S. 70

Green fees Mon.-Fri. £4.50 (subject to prior arrangement)
Weekends with member only

Professional Allan Dailey

Visiting societies April-Oct. £6 per head

Meals Lunch daily (except Mon.)

Nearest railway station Ascot 3 miles

Hotels in vicinity Berystede, Royal Berkshire and Royal Foresters, Ascot; Pennyhill Park and Cricketers', Bagshot

BETCHWORTH PARK (27)

Reigate Road, Dorking, Surrey

Tel: Dorking 2052

Founded 1924 750 members

18 holes 6,105 yards S.S.S. 69 Parkland

Green fees Mon.-Fri. Men £2 per rd. £2.50 per day
Ladies £1.50 per rd. £2 per day
Weekends with member only
Public holidays with member only
Visitors advised to telephone Secretary in advance

Professional A. King

Membership Full subscription £55 p.a. (E.F. £55)

Visiting societies Max. 45 Wed. and Thurs. only £4.50 per head (fully inc.)

Meals Lunch and tea available (except Mon.)

Nearest railway station Dorking 1½ miles

Hotels in vicinity Punch Bowl Motel and White Horse, Dorking

BISHOP'S STORTFORD (28)

Dunmow Road, Bishop's Stortford, Herts.

Tel: Bishop's Stortford 54715

Founded 1910 750 members

18 holes 6,212 yards S.S.S. 70 Parkland

Green fees Mon.-Fri. £2 per rd./day
Weekends with member only
Bona fide club members only, handicap cert. essential

Professional G. Aitken

Membership Full subscription £40 p.a. (E.F. £50)

Visiting societies Max. 40 £2 per head Catering as required

Meals Lunch and tea (except Mon.)
Buttery Bar—light snacks

Nearest railway station Bishop's Stortford 1 mile

Hotels in vicinity Foxley, Dane House, Railway and George, Bishop's Stortford

BLACKMOOR (29)

Whitehill, Bordon, Hants.

Tel: Bordon 2772

Founded 1913 500 members Venue for top amateur events

18 holes 6,202 yards S.S.S. 70 Heather and pine

Green fees Mon.-Fri. £2.50 per rd./day
Weekends £3.50 per rd./day
Introduction necessary

Professional A. White

Membership Full subscription £38 p.a. (E.F. £38)

Visiting societies Max. 60 (foursomes), otherwise 40
£5-6 per head

Meals Morning coffee, lunch, tea and high tea every day

Nearest railway station Liphook 4 miles, Liss 4½ miles

Hotels in vicinity Silver Birch, Blackmoor; Passfield Oak, Nr Liphook

BOGNOR REGIS (30)

Downview Road, Felpham, Bognor Regis, Sussex

Tel: Bognor 21929

Founded 1892 Course designed by James Braid
Venue for annual Purley Trophy
800 members

18 holes 6,308 yards S.S.S. 70 Flat parkland

Green fees Mon.-Fri. £1.50
Weekends £3

Professional H. T. Riseborough (tel: Bognor 5209)

Membership Full subscription £30 p.a. (E.F. £54)

Visiting societies Max. 24 Terms by arrangement

Meals By prior arrangement

Nearest railway station Bognor Regis 2 miles

Hotels in vicinity Royal Norfolk, Bognor Regis, Sussex

BOXMOOR (31)

Box Lane, Hemel Hempstead, Herts.

Tel: Hemel Hempstead 2434

Founded 1890 225 members

9 holes 4,328 yards S.S.S. 61 (18 tees) Very undulating

Green fees Mon.-Fri. 66p
Weekends no visitors

Membership Full subscription £16.50 p.a.

Visiting societies Max. 20 Green fee £1.32 per day
Catering by arrangement

Meals Bar snacks available

Nearest railway station Hemel Hempstead 1 mile

Hotels in vicinity Post House and Watermill, Hemel Hempstead

BOYCE HILL (32)

Vicarage Hill, Benfleet, Essex

Tel: South Benfleet 3625

18 holes 6,005 yards S.S.S. 69 Hilly parkland

Green fees Mon.-Fri. £1.50
Weekends with member only

Professional D. Slocombe

Visiting societies Terms by arrangement

Meals Lunch and tea

Nearest railway station Benfleet $1\frac{1}{2}$ miles

Hotels in vicinity Essex Centre, Basildon

BRAINTREE (33)

King's Lane, Stisted, Nr Braintree, Essex
Tel: Braintree 1117

Founded 1892 (9 holes) Increased to 18 holes 1973
485 members

18 holes 6,026 yards S.S.S. 69 Undulating parkland

Green fees Mon.-Fri. £1.65 per rd.
Weekends £2.20 per rd.

Professional Tony Parcell

Membership Full subscription £35 p.a. (E.F. £40)

Visiting societies 50 plus Terms negotiable

Meals All meals available (except Mon. and Wed.)

Nearest railway station Braintree 2 miles

Hotels in vicinity White Hart, Boar's Head and Horn, Braintree

BRAMLEY (34)

Gosden Hill, Bramley, Surrey
Tel: Bramley 2696

Founded 1913 700 members (approx.)

18 holes 5,855 yards S.S.S. 68 Picturesque parkland

Green fees Mon.-Fri. £2.20 per rd. £3.30 per day
Weekends no visitors

Professional V. Hood (tournament professional also)

Membership Full subscription £40 p.a. (E.F. £55)

Visiting societies Max. 60 Approx. £4.50 per head

Meals Meals available on request

Nearest railway station Guildford 3 miles

Hotels in vicinity Bramley Grange (½ mile from Club)

BRENT VALLEY (35)

Cuckoo Lane, off Church Road, Hanwell, London W7
Tel: 01-567 1287

18 holes 5,710 yards S.S.S. 67 Parkland

Green fees Mon.-Fri. 50p
Weekends 75p
Public course, no introduction necessary

Visiting societies Not catered for

Nearest railway station Ealing Broadway (B.R. and Central and District line tubes)

BRENTWOOD (36)

King George's Field, Ingrave Road, Brentwood, Essex

Tel: Brentwood 218714

18 holes 6,328 yards S.S.S. 70 Parkland

Green fees Mon.-Fri. 75p per rd.
Weekends £1
Municipal course, no introduction necessary

Professional A. Gowers

Visiting societies Terms on application

Nearest railway station Brentwood

Hotels in vicinity Lion & Lamb and Moat House, Brentwood

BRICKENDON GRANGE (37)

Brickendon, Nr Hertford, Herts.

Tel: Bayford 258

Founded 1964 650 members

18 holes 6,325 yards S.S.S. 70 Well-wooded parkland

Green fees Mon.-Fri. £2.50 per rd./day
Weekends £4 per rd./day
No introduction necessary but must be with member before 1 p.m. on Sun.

Professional R. J. Taylor (tel: Bayford 218)

Visiting societies Weekdays only Terms by arrangement

Meals Full catering available, by prior arrangement with the House Manager (tel: Bayford 228)

Nearest railway station Bayford Station 2 miles

Hotels in vicinity Salisbury Arms, Hertford

BRIGHTON & HOVE (38)

Dyke Road, Brighton, Sussex

Tel: Brighton 556482

Founded 1887 250 members

9 holes 5,535 yards S.S.S.67 Downland
Reduced to 9 holes in 1960 due to compulsory land purchase, but second 9 played from different tees

Green fees Mon.-Fri. £1 per rd.
Weekends £2 per rd.

Professional W. P. F. Brampton

Membership Full subscription £38 p.a. (E.F. £38)

Visiting societies Max 50 Green fee plus catering by arrangement

Meals Weekdays (except Tues.), to be ordered by 1 p.m.

Nearest railway station Brighton 5 miles

Hotels in vicinity Numerous hotels in Brighton area

BROMLEY (39)

Magpie Hall Lane, Bromley, Kent

Tel: 01-462 1297

9 holes 5,586 yards S.S.S. 66 Parkland

Green fees Public course, very reasonable charges
Visitors welcome at all times

Professional L. Wallis

Visiting societies Not catered for

Nearest railway station Bromley South

Hotels in vicinity Bromley Court, Bromley; Bickley Manor, Bickley

BROOKMANS PARK (40)

Brookmans Park, Hatfield, Herts.

Tel: Potters Bar 52487

Founded 1930 600 members

18 holes 6,436 yards S.S.S. 71 Parkland

Green fees Mon.-Fri. £2.75 per day
Weekends introduction by member only

Professional C. Christison

Membership Full subscription £50 p.a. (E.F. £100)

Visiting societies £5 per head By arrangement

Meals Full catering (except Mon.)

Nearest railway station Brookmans Park 1 mile

Hotels in vicinity Salisbury Arms, Hatfield; Esso Motel, South Mimms

BUCKINGHAM (41)

Radclive, Buckingham, Bucks.

Tel: Buckingham 3282

9 holes 5,772 yards S.S.S. 68

Green fees Mon.-Fri. £1.50 per day
Visiting societies Weekdays only
Terms on application
Nearest railway station

BURHILL (42)

Walton-on-Thames, Surrey
Tel: Walton-on-Thames 27345

18 holes 6,367 yards S.S.S. 70 Parkland
Green fees On application
Visiting societies Weekdays only
Meals Lunch daily
Nearest railway station Walton-on-Thames
Hotels in vicinity Ashley Park, Walton-on-Thames; Oatlands Park, Weybridge

BURNHAM BEECHES (43)

Green Lane, Burnham, Bucks.
Tel: Burnham 61448

Founded 1891 550 members
18 holes 6,360 yards S.S.S. 70 Undulating parkland
Green fees Mon.-Fri. £2.25 per rd. £3.30 per day
Weekends No visitors
Introduction necessary
Professional Joe Burnham
Membership Waiting list
Visiting societies Wed.-Fri. Max. 60 £5.50 per head, inc. VAT and grats.
Meals Lunch and tea (hot lunch to be ordered before 10 a.m.)
Nearest railway station Burnham 1 mile
Hotels in vicinity Burnham Beeches and Grovefield, Burnham

BURNHAM-ON-CROUCH (44)

Ferry Road, Creeksea, Burnham-on-Crouch, Essex
Tel: Maldon 782282

Founded 1923 350 members
9 holes 5,805 yards S.S.S. 68 Rising ground on north of river

Green fees Mon.-Fri. £1 per rd. £1.50 per day
Weekends £2 per rd.
50% reduction with member
No green fees Sat. and Sun. mornings

Membership Full subscription £20 p.a. (E.F. £20)

Visiting societies Tues. and Fri. only Charges as per green fees

Meals On request, except Mon.

Nearest railway station Burnham-on-Crouch

Hotels in vicinity Ye Olde White Harte, Burnham-on-Crouch

BURY ST EDMUNDS (45)

Westley Road, Fornham All Saints, Bury St Edmunds, Suffolk

Tel: Bury St Edmunds 5979

18 holes 6,615 yards S.S.S. 72 Well-wooded parkland

Green fees Mon.-Fri. £1.25 per rd.
Weekends £2.40 per rd.
Reduction with member

Visiting societies Max. 100 Weekdays only

Meals Full catering to order every day

Hotels in vicinity Angel, Suffolk and One Bull Inn, Bury St Edmunds

BUSH HILL PARK (46)

Bush Hill, Winchmore Hill, London N21

Tel: 01-360 5728

Founded 1895 600 members

18 holes 5,735 yards S.S.S. 67

Green fees Mon.-Fri. £2 per rd. (£1.25 with member)
£3 per day (£2 with member)
Weekends £2.50 per rd., by appointment only after 1 p.m.
Ladies' day Wed.

Professional G. Low

Membership Full subscription £55 p.a. (E.F. £50)

Visiting societies Tues., Thurs. and Fri. only
£5 per head inc. green fee, lunch and high tea

Meals Lunch and tea (to be ordered in advance if possible)

Nearest railway station Enfield Town and Enfield Chase, both ½ mile
Southgate (Piccadilly line tube) 2 miles

BUSHEY HALL (47)

Bushey, Watford, Herts.

Tel: Watford 25802

Founded 1886 450 members

18 holes 6,164 yards S.S.S. 69 Parkland

Green fees Mon.-Fri. £3 per day
Weekends with member only

Professional A. E. Rowland

Visiting societies Max. 50 Terms by arrangement

Meals Tea and snacks daily, lunches by arrangement

Nearest railway station Bushey and Oxhey (Bakerloo line tube) 1 mile

Hotels in vicinity Spider's Web, Bushey

CALCOT PARK (48)

Calcot, Reading, Berks.

Tel: Reading 27124

Founded 1930 400 members

18 holes 6,180 yards S.S.S. 69 Parkland

Green fees Mon.-Fri. £2.75
Weekends no visitors
Introduction necessary

Professional G. C. Norton

Membership Waiting list

Visiting societies Restricted. £5.25 per head by arrangement

Meals Daily (except Mon.)

Nearest railway station Reading 5 miles

Hotels in vicinity Post House, Reading; Copper Inn, Pangbourne

CAMBERLEY HEATH (49)

Golf Drive, Camberley, Surrey GU15 1JG

Tel: Camberley 23258

Founded 1913 650 members
Close military associations, in particular with Staff College, Sandhurst
Special facilities for British Airways Staff

18 holes 6,213 yards S.S.S. 70 Heathland with numerous pine trees

Green Fees Mon.-Fri. £2.70 per rd./day (with member £1 per rd. £1.70 per day)

Weekends £1.70 with member only
Bona fide club members with introduction

Professional Harry Adams

Membership Full subscription £40 p.a. (E.F. £40) plus VAT

Visiting societies Max. 60 £5 approx. per head

Meals Lunch and tea (except Mon.), bar snacks available at all times

Nearest railway station Camberley $1\frac{1}{2}$ miles

Hotels in vicinity Frimley Hall, Camberley

CANON'S BROOK (50)

Elizabeth Way, Harlow, Essex

Tel: Harlow 21482

18 holes 6,793 yards S.S.S. 73 Parkland

Green fees Bona fide club members accepted without introduction
Mon. and weekends, with member only

Visiting societies Not Mon. Terms on application

Meals Full catering every day

Nearest railway station Harlow Town

Hotels in vicinity Saxon Inn Motel and Churchgate Inn, Harlow

Canterbury cathedral

CANTERBURY (51)

Scotland Hills, Canterbury, Kent

Tel: Canterbury 63586

18 holes 6,222 yards S.S.S. 70 Woodland

Green fees Mon.-Fri. £1.75 per rd.
Weekends £2.25 per rd.
No reservation or introduction necessary with the exception of Sun. a.m.

Visiting societies Tues., Wed. and Thurs. only. Terms by arrangement

Meals Lunch daily (4 hours' notice requested)

Nearest railway station Canterbury

Hotels in vicinity George & Dragon, Fordwich; Chaucer, Canterbury

CHELMSFORD (52)

Widford, Chelmsford, Essex

Tel: Chelmsford 56483

18 holes 5,912 yards S.S.S. 68 Parkland

Green fees Mon.-Fri. visitors welcome. Must produce cert. of handicap if not playing with member
Weekends with member only

Visiting societies Weekdays only

Meals Lunch daily (except Mon.)

Nearest railway station Chelmsford

Hotels in vicinity Lion & Lamb, Brentwood; County, Chelmsford

CHESHAM & LEY HILL (53)

The Clubhouse, Ley Hill, Chesham, Bucks.

Tel: Chesham 4541

Founded 1919 250 members

9 holes 4,925 yards S.S.S. 63 Common land

Green fees Mon.-Fri. £1
Introduction necessary

Membership Full subscription £20 p.a. (E.F. £20)

Visiting societies Not catered for

Meals Limited facilities, by prior arrangement only

Nearest railway station Chesham (Metropolitan line tube)

Hotels in vicinity Crown and Swan, Ley Hill

CHESTERFIELD (54)

Whitstable, Kent

Tel: Chesterfield 2243

Founded 1924 One of the oldest clubhouses in the country, with excellent view of Thames estuary

18 holes 6,218 yards S.S.S. 70 Clay surface

Green fees On application
Visitors welcome; after 11 a.m. on Sun.

Professional M. Waldron

Membership New members welcome. Fees on application

Visiting societies By arrangement

Meals Mon.-Sat. by prior arrangement with the Steward
No catering on Sun.

Nearest railway station Whitstable 1½ miles

Hotels in vicinity Marine, Tankerton

CHIGWELL (55)

High Road, Chigwell, Essex

Tel: 01-500 2059

Founded 1925 700 members

18 holes 6,283 yards S.S.S. 70 Parkland

Green fees Mon.-Fri. £2 per rd. £3 per day
Weekends no visitors
Must be members of club

Professional E. E. Whitcombe

Visiting societies Weekdays only. Charges on request

Meals Available all times (except Mon.)

Nearest railway station Chigwell (Central line tube) ¼ mile

Hotels in vicinity Roebuck, Buckhurst Hill

CHINGFORD (56)

158 Station Road, Chingford, Essex

Tel: 01-529 3597

18 holes S.S.S. 67 Public course

Green fees Visitors welcome all week
(Red coats must be worn)

Professional L. and R. Gowers

Nearest railway station Chingford

CHIPSTEAD (57)

How Lane, Coulsdon, Surrey

Tel: Downland 55781

18 holes 5,416 yards S.S.S. 66 Downland

Green fees Mon.-Fri. £1.60 per rd.
Weekends £1.35 (with member only)
Bona fide club members only

Professional J. Hudson

Visiting societies Catered for except Tues. and Thurs.

Meals Full catering (except Thurs.)

Nearest railway station Chipstead

CHISLEHURST (58)

Camden Place, Chislehurst, Kent BR7 5HJ

Tel: 01-467 2782

Founded 1898 Clubhouse of historical interest 700 members

18 holes 5,128 yards S.S.S. 65 Heather and woodland

Green fees Mon.-Fri. £1.65 per day
Weekends no visitors

Professional D. J. Pratt

Membership Full subscription £51 p.a. (E.F. £51)

Visiting societies Max. 40 £6 per head

Meals By prior arrangement

Nearest railway station Chislehurst ½ mile

Hotels in vicinity Bull, Chislehurst; Bromley Court and Hackwood, Bromley

CHORLEYWOOD (59)

Common Road, Chorley Wood, Herts.

Tel: Chorleywood 2009

Founded 1891 300 members

9 holes 5,676 yards S.S.S. 67 Flat parkland

Green fees Mon.-Fri. £1.25 (not Tues.)
Weekends £2.75 (after 11.30 a.m.)

Visiting societies Weekdays except Tues. Terms by arrangement

Meals By prior arrangement

Nearest railway station Chorleywood (Metropolitan line tube) 2 miles

Hotels in vicinity Sportsman, Chorleywood

CLACTON-ON-SEA (60)

West Road, Clacton-on-Sea, Essex CO15 1AJ

Tel: Clacton 21919

Founded 1908 450 members

18 holes 6,097 yards S.S.S. 69 Marsh land, close to sea

Green fees Mon.-Fri. £1.65 per rd. £2 per day
Weekends £2 per rd./day
Introduction necessary

Professional Chris Walley

Membership Full subscription £32.50 p.a. (E.F. £32.50)

Visiting societies Max. 50 Charges as per green fees

Meals Available

Nearest railway station Clacton-on-Sea 2 miles

Hotels in vicinity Royal, Clacton-on-Sea

COODEN BEACH (61)

Cooden Sea Road, Bexhill-on-Sea, Sussex

Tel: Cooden 2040

Founded 1912

18 holes 6,388 yards S.S.S. 70 Seaside

Green fees Mon.-Fri. £2 per rd./day
Weekends £2.50 per rd./day

Professional Ron Southall

Visiting societies Weekdays only. Terms by arrangement

Meals Lunch and tea every day (except Mon.)

Nearest railway station Cooden Beach 150 yards

Hotels in vicinity Cooden Beach, Bexhill-on-Sea

COOMBE HILL (62)

Golf Club Drive, Kingston Hill, Surrey KT2 7DG

Tel: 01-942 2284

Founded 1911 650 members

18 holes 6,429 yards Sandy soil, every fairway tree-lined

Green fees £3.50
Introduction by member only

Professional Ken Bousfield

Visiting societies £7.50 per head (inc. VAT)
Only 12 societies admitted per year

Meals Lunch and tea every day

Nearest railway station New Malden 1 mile

Hotels in vicinity Fairmile, Cobham; Griffin, Kingston-upon-Thames

Comment Since 1911 four professionals at the club have become Open Champions: Sandy (Alex) Herd, Arthur Havers, Henry Cotton and Dick Burton. Archie Compston was also professional here.

COOMBE WOOD (63)

George Road, Kingston Hill, Surrey KT2 7DG

Tel: 01-942 0388

18 holes 5,198 yards S.S.S. 66 Parkland

Green fees Mon.-Fri £2.30
Weekends with member only

Professional W. B. Murray

Visiting societies Terms by arrangement

Nearest railway station New Malden

Meals Lunch daily (except Mon.)

COPTHORNE (64)

Copthorne Bank, Crawley, Sussex

Tel: Copthorne 2033

18 holes 5,727 yards S.S.S. 67 Wooded heathland course with natural greens

Green fees Mon.-Fri. visitors welcome
Weekends members of recognised clubs only
Charges on application

Visiting societies Weekdays only Terms by arrangement
Advance booking necessary

Meals Lunch every day (except Fri.), to be ordered in advance

Nearest railway station Crawley

Hotels in vicinity Ye Olde Felbridge, East Grinstead; Chequers, Horley

CORHAMPTON (65)

Corhampton, Nr Droxford, Hants.

Tel: Droxford 279

Founded 1890 350 members

9 holes 5,930 yards S.S.S. 68 Downland

Green fees Mon.-Fri. £1.50 per rd.
Weekends £3 per rd.
50% reduction with member

Professional R. E. Crockford

Membership Full subscription £21 p.a. (E.F. £21)

Visiting societies Restricted. Terms by arrangement

Meals Tea (Sat. and Sun., summer only)

Nearest railway station Botley 8 miles

Hotels in vicinity Numerous hotels in Southampton area

COULSDON COURT (66)

Coulsdon Road, Coulsdon, Surrey

Tel: 01-660 0468

18 holes 6,045 yards S.S.S. 69 Parkland

Green fees Mon.-Fri. £1
Weekends £1.35
Advisable to book for weekend starting time

Visiting societies Not usually catered for. Terms by arrangement

Meals Lunch daily

Nearest railway station Coulsdon

COWDRAY PARK (67)

Midhurst, Sussex

Tel: Midhurst 3599

Founded 1904 735 members

18 holes 6,174 yards S.S.S. 69 Sandy soil, playable throughout the year. Magnificent scenery with expansive views over the South Downs

Green fees Mon.-Fri. £1.65 per rd./day
Weekends £3.30 per rd./day

Professional Jimmy Thomson
Membership Full subscription £22 p.a. (E.F. £22)
Visiting societies Max. 24 Society rate £4.50 per head
Meals Full catering available (except Fri.)
Nearest railway station Haslemere approx. 7 miles
Hotels in vicinity Angel and Spread Eagle, Midhurst

CREWS HILL (68)

Cattlegate Road, Crews Hill, Enfield, Middx.
Tel: 01-363 0787

18 holes 6,122 yards S.S.S. 69 Parkland
Green fees Mon.-Sat. visitors welcome
Sun. with member only
Visiting societies Weekdays only
Meals Lunch daily
Nearest railway station Enfield Town
Hotels in vicinity West Lodge Park, Barnet

CROHAM HURST (69)

Croham Road, South Croydon, Surrey
Tel: 01-657 2075

Founded 1911 800 members
18 holes 6,274 yards (5,736 metres) S.S.S. 70 Parkland
Green fees £2.20 per rd. £3.30 per day
Bona fide club members only
Professional R. Robson
Membership Full subscription £62.50 p.a. (E.F. £62.50)
Visiting societies Max. 60 £5 per head all day
Meals Lunch and tea every day
Nearest railway station South Croydon
Hotels in vicinity Selsdon Park, Sanderstead; Swiss Echoes

CROWBOROUGH BEACON (70)

Crowborough, Sussex
Tel: Crowborough 61511 and 4106

Founded 1895 600 members
18 holes 6,295 yards S.S.S. 70 Forest turf, heather and gorse

Green fees Mon.-Fri. £2.25
Weekends £3.25 (after 3 p.m.)
Visitors must be bona fide club members

Professional P. Broadbent

Membership Full subscription £40 p.a. (E.F. £40) plus VAT

Visiting societies Max. 40 £4 per head

Meals Lunch and tea (except Mon.)

Nearest railway station Crowborough 3 miles

Hotels in vicinity Crest and Beacon Hill, Crowborough

CUDDINGTON (71)

Banstead Road, Banstead, Surrey

Tel: 01-393 0952

Founded 1929 845 members

18 holes 6,448 yards S.S.S. 71 Chalk subsoil, parkland

Green fees Weekdays £2 per day (plus VAT)
Weekends £3 per rd.
Public hols. £3 per rd.
Visitors must have letter of introduction and club handicap

Professional Harold Guy

Meals Lunch and tea every day

Membership Subscription £42 plus VAT (E.F. 1½ times sub)
Waiting list

Visiting societies Thurs. only. Daily charges £5.75-£6.50.

Nearest railway station Banstead 250 yards

Hotels in vicinity Drift Bridge and Linden House, Epsom

DARTFORD (72)

The Clubhouse, Dartford Heath, Dartford, Kent

Tel: Dartford 23616

18 holes 6,029 yards S.S.S. 69 Heathland

Green fees Mon.-Fri. £2.25 per day
Weekends with member only

Professional K. Alcorn

Visiting societies Terms on application

Meals Lunch daily (to be ordered in advance)

Nearest railway station Dartford

Hotels in vicinity Bull, Birchwood

DATCHET (73)

Datchet, Nr Slough, Bucks.

Tel: Slough 43887

Founded 1890 350 members

9 holes 5,902 yards S.S.S. 68 Alternative tees at some holes

Green fees Mon.-Fri. £1.65 per day (£1 with member)
Weekends £1.65 with member only

Professional A. F. Bolton

Membership Full subscription £27 p.a. (E.F. £27)

Visiting societies None

Meals Snacks at bar only

Nearest railway station Datchet 5 minutes' walk

Hotels in vicinity Manor, Datchet; Castle, Windsor

Eton College.

DENHAM (74)

Tilehouse Lane, Denham, Bucks.

Tel: Denham 2022

Founded 1908 550 members

18 holes 6,387 yards S.S.S. 71

Green fees Mon.-Fri. £2.20 per rd. £3.30 per day
Weekends with member only

Professional J. Sheridan

Membership Full subscription £66 p.a. (E.F. £100)

Visiting societies Tues.-Thurs. only. £5.50 per head inc.

Meals Weekdays only, to be ordered by 10.30 a.m.

Nearest railway station Denham

Hotels in vicinity Bull, Gerrard's Cross; Bell House, Beaconsfield

DORKING (75)

Chart Park, Dorking, Surrey

Tel: Dorking 5714

Founded 1897 350 members

9 holes 5,006 yards S.S.S. 64 (2nd 9 holes played from different tees)

Green Fees £1 per rd.
Must be introduced and play with member

Professional E. Barnes

Membership Waiting list

Visiting societies Max. 30 £3 per head, meals extra by arrangement

Meals Snack lunch and tea; dinner by arrangement

Nearest railway station Dorking

Hotels in vicinity White Horse and Burford Bridge, Dorking

Comments Situated close to Box Hill, a Surrey beauty spot

DULWICH & SYDENHAM HILL (76)

Grange Lane, College Road, London SE21

Tel: 01-693 1221

Founded 1893 Peter Oosterhuis began golf as a member here, and was still attached to the club in his formative years as a professional. 750 members

18 holes 6,019 yards S.S.S. 69

Green fees Mon.-Fri. £2 per rd. £3 per day
Weekends with member only
Visitors must be bona fide club members

Professional Len Rowe

Membership Full subscription £45 p.a. (E.F. £45)

Visiting societies Max. 20 (approx.)
Average £6 per head, depending on requirements

Meals Lunch and tea available every day

Nearest railway station Sydenham Hill 5 mins.

Hotels in vicinity Queen's, Crystal Palace

DUNSTABLE DOWNS (77)

Whipsnade Road, Dunstable, Beds.

Tel: Dunstable 63634

18 holes 6,184 yards S.S.S. 69 Downland

Green fees Mon.-Fri. £1.65 per rd. £2.20 per day
Weekends reduced, with member only
Bona fide club members only

Professional G. Macarthy

Visiting societies Very welcome Thurs. and Fri. only
Terms by arrangement

Meals Full catering Wed.-Sun., reduced Mon. and Tues.

Nearest railway station Luton 5 miles

Hotels in vicinity Old Sugar Loaf and Old Palace Lodge, Dunstable

DYKE (78)

Dyke Road, Brighton, Sussex

Tel: Pynings 230

Founded 1911 600 members

18 holes 6,411 yards S.S.S. 71 Downland

Green fees Mon.-Fri. £2 per rd.
Sat. £1.75 per rd. £2.50 per day
Sun. £2 after 12 noon

Professional Paul Longmore

Membership Full subscription £42 p.a. (E.F. £50)

Visiting societies Max. 40 £5 per head

Meals Lunch (to be booked before 10 a.m.)

Nearest railway station Brighton 5 miles

Hotels in vicinity Numerous hotels in Brighton

DYRHAM PARK (79)

Galley Lane, Barnet, Herts.

Tel: 01-440 3361

18 holes 6,450 yards S.S.S. 71 Parkland

Green fees Visitors must be introduced and play with a member at all times

Professional J. Adams

Visiting societies Terms on application

Meals Catering facilities available

Nearest railway station High Barnet (Northern line tube)

Hotels in vicinity Esso Motel, Barnet

EALING (80)

Perivale Lane, Greenford, Middx.

Tel: 01-997 0937

Founded 1898 500 members

18 holes 6,118 yards S.S.S. 69 Parkland, with River Brent running through the course

Green fees Mon.-Fri. £3.30 per day
Weekends £4.40 per day (reduction with member)
Introduction preferred

Professional Arnold and Owen Stickley

Visiting societies Terms on application

Meals Lunch and tea daily

Nearest railway station Ealing 2 miles

Hotels in vicinity Carnarvon, Ealing Common

EAST BERKS (81)

Ravenswood Avenue, Crowthorne, Berks.

Tel: Crowthorne 2041

Founded 1904 600 members

18 holes 6,324 yards S.S.S. 70 Heathland

Green fees Mon.-Fri. £3 per day min.
Weekends no visitors
Introduction and club certificate necessary

Professional Mick Notley

Membership Full subscription £36 p.a. (E.F. £36)

Visiting societies Thurs. and Fri. only £5.50 per head

Meals A la carte every day

Nearest railway station Crowthorne

Hotels in vicinity Waterloo, Crowthorne; Berystede and Royal Foresters, Ascot

EAST BRIGHTON (82)

Roedean Road, Brighton, Sussex

Tel: Brighton 64838

18 holes 6,179 yards S.S.S. 69 Seaside, downland

Green fees Mon.-Fri. £1.75 per rd. £2.50 per day
Weekends £2 per rd. £3 per day
Bona fide club members welcome without reservation

Professional C. Parsons

Visiting societies Midweek only, terms by arrangement
Meals Lunch and tea daily (except Mon.)
Nearest railway station Brighton
Hotels in vicinity Numerous hotels in Brighton

Brighton: Regency Square

EAST HERTS (83)

Hamels Park, Puckeridge, Nr Ware, Herts.
Tel: Ware 821978

Founded 1898 (moved to new course June 1974) 550 members
18 holes 6,400 yards S.S.S. 70 Parkland
Green fees Mon.-Fri. £1
Weekends £2
Introduction necessary
Professional J. Hamilton
Membership Full subscription £40 p.a. (E.F. £40)
Visiting societies Terms on application to the Secretary
Meals Full catering
Nearest railway station Ware
Hotels in vicinity Cannons, Ware

EASTBOURNE DOWNS (84)

East Dean Road, Eastbourne, Sussex

Tel: Eastbourne 20827

18 holes 6,623 yards S.S.S. 72 Downland

Green fees Mon.-Fri. £1.50 per day
Weekends £1.80 per day

Professional F. Wooller

Visiting societies Certain restrictions. Terms by arrangement

Meals Lunch daily (to be ordered in advance)

Nearest railway station Eastbourne

Hotels in vicinity Numerous hotels in Eastbourne

EFFINGHAM (85)

Effingham, Surrey

Tel: Bookham 52203/4

Founded 1928 1,000 members (inc. squash, tennis etc.)

18 holes 6,598 yards S.S.S. 71 Chalk and downland course

Green fees Mon.-Fri. £2.50 (£1.50 after 2 p.m.)
Sat. only £3 (£2 after 2 p.m.)

Professional P. E. Loxley

Visiting societies Wed.-Fri. every week between April and October
£6 per head

Meals Lunch and tea every day

Nearest railway station Effingham Junction 2 miles

Hotels in vicinity Thatchers, Preston Cross and Bookham Grange

ELLESBOROUGH (86)

Butlers Cross, Nr Aylesbury, Bucks.

Tel: Wendover 2114

Founded 1906 Then a 9-hole course on slopes of Chilterns, part of the Chequers estate. 1929 enlarged to 18 holes
650 members

18 holes 6,215 yards S.S.S. 70 Parkland

Green fees Mon.-Fri. £2.50 per rd./day
Weekends with members only

Professional D. O. Creamer

Membership Full subscription £44 p.a. (E.F. £44)
Ladies' full subscription £33 p.a. (E.F. £44)
Waiting list for all categories of male membership

Visiting societies Wed. and Thurs. only. £4.50 per head, inc.
Meals Available all week except Mon. (24 hours' notice is desirable)
Nearest railway station Wendover 1½ miles
Hotels in vicinity Red Lion and Shoulder of Mutton, Wendover

ELTHAM WARREN (87)

Bexley Road, Eltham, London SE9
Tel: 01-850 4477

9 holes 5,820 yards S.S.S. 68 Parkland
Green fees Mon.-Fri. £1.75 per rd.
Weekends with member only
Professional P. Tickle
Visiting societies Not usually catered for
Meals Bar snacks available
Nearest railway station Eltham Park 5 minutes' walk
Hotels in vicinity Yorkshire Grey, Eltham Green

ELY CITY (88)

Cambridge Road, Ely, Cambs.
Tel: Ely 2751

Founded 1961 500 members
18 holes 6,677 yards S.S.S. 72 Undulating, with lakes and picturesque views of Cathedral
Green fees Mon.-Fri. £1.50 (£1 with member)
Weekends £2.50 (£1.50 with member)
Professional F. C. Rowden
Hugh Baiocchi (tournaments)
Membership Full subscription £30 p.a. (E.F. £60 plus VAT)
Visiting societies Max. 80-100 Charges as per green fees of the day
Meals Always available
Nearest railway station Ely 1½ miles
Hotels in vicinity Lamb, Ely

ENFIELD (89)

Old Park Road, Windmill Hill, Enfield, Middx.
Tel: 01-363 3970

Founded 1893 675 members
18 holes 6,120 yards S.S.S. 69 Undulating parkland

Green fees By arrangement
Professional R. F. Jonas
Visiting societies Terms by arrangement
Meals Lunch and tea (except Mon.—bar snacks only)
Nearest railway station Enfield Chase ½ mile
Hotels in vicinity Old Park Heights, Royal Chase and Holtwhites, Enfield

EPSOM (90)

Longdown Lane South, Epsom, Surrey
Tel: Epsom 21666

Founded 1889 One of the oldest clubs in Surrey
18 holes 5,535 yards S.S.S. 67 Downland
Green fees Mon.-Fri. 75p
Weekends £1.50
Professional V. A. Ruddle (tel: 26829)
Visiting societies Max. 25 Green fees plus catering by arrangement
Meals Bar snacks only
Nearest railway station Epsom Downs 200 yards
Hotels in vicinity Epsom Downs and Linden House, Epsom

FARNHAM (91)

Sands, Farnham, Surrey
Tel: Runfold 2109

Founded 1896 600 members
18 holes 6,254 yards S.S.S. 70 Sandy, parkland and heath
Green fees Mon.-Fri. £2.20 per rd. £3.30 per day (inc. VAT)
Weekends with member only
Professional R. L. Hammond
Membership Subscription £38 p.a. (E.F. £45)
Visiting societies Wed. and Thurs. only. £4.50 per day inc.
Meals All meals available daily
Nearest railway station Farnham 2 miles
Hotels in vicinity Hog's Back and Bush, Farnham

FAVERSHAM (92)

Belmont Park, Faversham, Kent
Tel: Eastling 275

18 holes 6,053 yards S.S.S. 69 Parkland

Green fees Mon.-Fri. £1.65 per rd.
Weekends £2.50 per rd.

Professional D. Place

Visiting societies Max. 20 Tues. and Sat. only

Meals Lunch and tea daily (except Fri.). Prior booking requested

Nearest railway station Faversham 3 miles

Hotels in vicinity Ship, Faversham

FINCHLEY (93)

Nether Court, Frith Lane, London NW7 1PU

Tel: 01-346 2436

Founded 1929 Course designed by James Braid

18 holes 6,402 yards S.S.S. 71 Parkland

Green fees Mon.-Fri. £2 per rd./day (plus VAT)
Sat. (after 12.30 p.m.) £3.50 (plus VAT)
Sun. (after 12.30 p.m.) £4 (plus VAT)

Professional D. Brown (tel: 01-346 5086)

Membership Waiting list

Visiting societies £2.50 per head (catering by arrangement)

Meals Lunch and tea (except Mon.). Bar snacks available

Nearest railway station Mill Hill East 1 mile, or Finchley Central 2 miles (Northern line tube)

Hotels in vicinity Hendon Hall

FLACKWELL HEATH (94)

High Wycombe, Bucks. HP10 9PE

Tel: Bourne End 20929

Founded 1920 600 members

18 holes 6,201 yards S.S.S. 70

Green fees Mon.-Fri. £2.20 per rd. (£1.10 with member)
Weekends with member only
Introduction necessary

Professional R. O. Trapp

Visiting societies Restricted, apply to Secretary

Meals Available weekdays only, to be ordered in advance

Nearest railway station High Wycombe

Hotels in vicinity George, Beaconsfield

FRILFORD HEATH (95)

Frilford Heath, Abingdon, Oxon.

Tel: Abingdon 228

Founded 1908 880 members

36 holes Red: 6,747 yards S.S.S. 72
Green: 6,019 yards S.S.S. 69
Heathland with abundance of heather and gorse

Green fees Mon.-Fri. £2.50
Weekends £3
Weekend visitors by arrangement only

Professional H. C. Rule

Membership Full subscription £45 p.a. (E.F. £45)

Visiting societies Max. 50 £5 approx. per head

Meals Lunch and tea every day

Nearest railway station Oxford 7 miles

Hotels in vicinity Upper Reaches, Abingdon; Randolph, Oxford

FRINTON-ON-SEA (96)

The Club House, The Esplanade, Frinton-on-Sea, Essex CO13 9EP

Tel: Frinton 4216

Founded 1896 780 members Course redesigned in 1929

18 holes 6,249 yards S.S.S. 70 Sub-soil clay and peat, fibrous turf

Green fees Mon.-Fri. £1.50 plus VAT
Weekends £2 plus VAT
Public hols. £2 plus VAT
Letter of introduction necessary

Professional Ray Hall

Membership Full subscription £32 p.a. (E.F. £25)

Visiting societies Weekdays only. Charges as per green fees

Meals All available

Nearest railway station Frinton-on-Sea 1 mile

Hotels in vicinity Frinton Lodge, Grand, Maplin, Glencoe Country Club and Cedars, Frinton-on-Sea

FULWELL (97)

Hampton Hill, Middx. TW12 1JY

Tel: 01-977 2733

Founded 1904 Frequently the venue for Southern Area P.G.A. Championships 300 members

18 holes 6,490 yards (5,935 metres) S.S.S. 71 Parkland

Green fees Mon.-Fri. £2.50 per rd./day
Weekends £4 per rd./day
Introduction necessary. Visitors must be bona fide members of other clubs

Professional 'Bill' Cox

Membership Full subscription £63.50 p.a. (E.F. £40)
Waiting list

Visiting societies Max. 50 £4.50 per head, plus grats.

Meals Lunch and tea daily (except Mon.), high tea or dinner if ordered before play. Lunch and dinner à la carte

Nearest railway station Fulwell 200 yards

Hotels in vicinity Richmond Hill and Richmond Gate, Richmond

GATTON MANOR (98)

Ockley, Nr Dorking, Surrey

Tel: Oakwood Hill 297

18 holes 6,903 yards S.S.S. 72 Parkland

Green fees Mon.-Fri. £1.10 per rd./day
Weekends £2.20 per rd./day
Visitors welcome at all times

Professional P. Gill

Visiting societies Mon.-Sat. Terms by arrangement

Meals Light lunch and bar snacks

Nearest railway station Ockley

Hotels in vicinity Gatton Manor

GERRARD'S CROSS (99)

Chalfont Park, Gerrard's Cross, Bucks.

Tel: Gerrard's Cross 83263

Founded 1924 500 members

18 holes 6,305 yards S.S.S. 70 Well-wooded parkland

Green fees Mon.-Fri. £2.75 (85p with member)
Weekends with member only

Professional Alasdair Barr

Membership Full subscription £73 p.a. (E.F. £100)

Visiting societies Thurs. and Fri. only. Max. 50 £4.75 per head (inc. VAT)

Meals Available at all times

Nearest railway station Gerrard's Cross 1 mile

Hotels in vicinity Bull, Gerrard's Cross; Bell House, Beaconsfield

GILLINGHAM (100)

Woodlands Road, Gillingham, Kent

Tel: Medway 53017

Founded 1909 680 members

18 holes 6,035 yards

Green fees Mon.-Fri. £1.20 per rd.
Weekends £1 with member

Professional Stan Barrow

Membership Subscription £33 p.a. (E.F. £36)
Ladies £25 p.a. (E.F. £20)

Visiting societies £1.20 per head (meals by arrangement)

Meals Available at all times

Nearest railway station Gillingham 2 miles

Hotels in vicinity Park

GIRTON (101)

Dodford Lane, Girton, Cambridge CB3 OQE

Tel: Cambridge 76169

Founded 1936 330 members

9 holes 6,418 yards S.S.S. 71 Flat moorland

Green fees Mon.-Fri. £1.50
Weekends £2
Visitors welcome, must be club members

Professional Chris Reed

Membership Full subscription £20 p.a. (E.F. £20)

Visiting societies Charges as per green fees of the day, by arrangement with the Secretary

Meals By arrangement with the Stewardess

Nearest railway station Cambridge

Hotels in vicinity University Arms and Garden House, Cambridge

Clare College, Cambridge

GOG MAGOG (102)

Babraham Road, Cambridge

Tel: Cambridge 47626

18 holes 6,286 yards S.S.S. 70 Parkland, sparsely wooded

Green fees On application to the Secretary

Professional R. Cox

Visiting societies Weekdays only. Terms by arrangement

Meals Lunch all week (prior booking requested)

Nearest railway station Cambridge

Hotels in vicinity Numerous hotels in Cambridge

GOODWOOD (103)

Goodwood, Nr Chichester, Sussex

Tel: Chichester 527491

18 holes 6,110 yards S.S.S. 69 Downland

Green fees Mon.-Fri. £1.50
Weekends £3
Bona fide club members welcomed

Professional K. Dash

Visiting societies Weekdays only, terms by arrangement

Meals Lunch and tea every day (except Mon.), to be ordered in advance

Nearest railway station Chichester

Hotels in vicinity Richmond Arms, Goodwood; Dolphin & Anchor, Chichester

Chichester Cathedral

GORING & STREATLEY (104)

Rectory Road, Streatley-on-Thames, Berks.
Tel: Goring 2688

Founded 1890 650 members

18 holes 6,232 yards S.S.S. 70 Parkland

Green fees Mon.-Fri. £2.20
Weekends £1.65 with member only

Professional Roy Mason

Visiting societies Weekdays only. Approx. £4 per head

Meals Lunch and tea daily (except Tues.)

Nearest railway station Goring $1\frac{1}{2}$ miles

Hotels in vicinity Miller of Mansfield, Goring; Bull, Streatley

GRIM'S DYKE (105)

Oxhey Lane, Hatch End, Pinner, Middx. HA5 4AL
Tel: 01-428 4093

Founded 1910 600 members

18 holes 5,598 yards S.S.S. 67 Parkland

Green fees Mon.-Fri. £2.20 per rd. £3.30 per day
Weekends with members only

Professional T. E. Adams

Membership Full subscription £52 p.a. (E.F. £55)

Visiting societies By arrangement with the Secretary (tel: 01-428 4539)

Meals Lunch, tea and bar snacks daily (lunch to be booked in advance)

Nearest railway station Hatch End

Hotels in vicinity King's Head, Harrow; Grim's Dyke Country and Old Redding, Harrow Weald

GUILDFORD (106)

High Path Road, Merrow, Guildford, Surrey
Tel: Guildford 63941

Founded 1886 450 members

18 holes 6,082 yards S.S.S. 70 Natural downland with views across the town

Green fees Mon.-Fri. £2 per rd.
Weekends with member only

Professional T. M. Turner

Membership Full subscription £40 p.a. (E.F. £40)
Waiting list

Visiting societies Max. 40 £4.25 per head, fully inc.

Meals Every day (except Mon.)

Nearest railway station Guildford 2 miles

Hotels in vicinity Many in town centre

HADLEY WOOD (107)

Beech Hill, Nr Barnet, Middx.

Tel: 01-449 4328

Founded 1922 600 members

18 holes 6,421 yards S.S.S. 71 Parkland

Green fees Mon.-Fri. £2.20 per rd. £3.30 per day
Weekends no visitors
Introduction required

Professional David Levermore

Visiting societies Max. 80 Wed. and Thurs. only. £6 per head approx.

Menu Full menu available

Nearest railway station Cockfosters (Piccadilly line tube) 3 miles
Hadley Wood $1\frac{1}{2}$ miles

Hotels in vicinity West Lodge Park, Hadley Wood

HAINAULT FOREST (108)

Chigwell Row, Hainault, Essex

Tel: 01-500 4178

36 holes No. 1: 5,754 yards S.S.S. 67
No. 2: 6,445 yards S.S.S. 71
Parkland courses close to Epping Forest, fairly hilly

Green fees On application

Professional E. Frost

Membership This is a private club on courses owned and controlled by the G.L.C. Terms on application

Visiting societies Not catered for

Meals Light meals available

Nearest railway station Hainault (Central line tube)

HAM MANOR (109)

Angmering, Littlehampton, Sussex BN16 4JE

Tel: Rustington 3288

Founded 1936

18 holes 6,216 yards S.S.S. 70 Gently undulating parkland

Green fees Mon.-Fri. £2.20 (with member £1.10)
Weekends £3 (with member £1.35)

Professional Tommy Horton

Visiting societies Weekdays only

Meals Lunch and tea (except Mon., snacks only)

Nearest railway station Angmering 1 mile

Hotels in vicinity Beach, Littlehampton; Broadmark, Rustington

HAMPSTEAD (110)

Winnington Road, London N2 OTU

Tel: 01-455 6420

Founded 1894 450 members

9 holes 5,812 yards S.S.S. 68

Green fees Mon.-Fri. £1.65 per rd./day
Weekends £3.30
Introduction necessary

Professional Terry Le Brocq

Membership Waiting list

Visiting societies Not catered for

Meals To order

Nearest railway station Golders Green (Northern line tube)

HANKLEY COMMON (111)

Tilford, Farnham, Surrey

Tel: Frenshaw 2493

Founded 1896 350 members

18 holes 6,509 yards S.S.S. 71

Green fees Mon.-Fri. £2.20 (with member £1.10)
Weekends £3.85 (with member £1.65)
Introduction necessary

Professional A. Macdonald

Membership Full subscription £46 plus VAT (E.F. £60 plus VAT)

Visiting societies Max. 50 Weds. only. £5.50 per head

Meals Every day (except Fri.), meals to be ordered before play

Nearest railway station Farnham 3½ miles

Hotels in vicinity Pride of the Valley and Frensham Pond, Churt

HAREWOOD DOWNS (112)

Chalfont St Giles, Bucks.
Tel: Little Chalfont 2308

18 holes S.S.S. 68 Parkland course

Green fees Mon.-Fri. £1.65 per rd. £2.20 per day (reductions if playing with member)
Weekends 85p with member only

Professional G. J. Pook

Visiting societies Terms by arrangement

Meals Lunch every day (except Mon.)

Nearest railway station Chalfont & Latimer (B.R. and Metropolitan line tube)

Hotels in vicinity King's Arms, Amersham

HARPENDEN (113)

Hammonds End, Redbourn Lane, Harpenden, Herts.
Tel: Harpenden 2580

Founded 1931 750 members

18 holes 6,223 yards S.S.S. 70 Parkland

Green fees Mon.-Fri. Charges on application
Weekends no visitors
Introduction required

Professional F. Robson (tel: Harpenden 4936)

Membership Waiting list

Visiting societies By arrangement

Meals Full catering (except Mon.)

Nearest railway station Harpenden 3 miles

Hotels in vicinity Moat House and Glen Eagle, Harpenden

HARPENDEN COMMON (114)

East Common, Harpenden, Herts. AL5 1BL
Tel: Harpenden 2856

Founded 1931 Course first constructed 1895 600 members

18 holes 5,500 yards S.S.S. 67

Green fees Mon.-Fri. £1.35 per rd. £2 per day
Weekends must be introduced by member

Professional S. R. Jackson

Membership Subscription Men £26 p.a.
Ladies £19 p.a. (E.F. £25)

Visiting societies By permission of the Committee
Meals Available at all times
Nearest railway station Harpenden 1 mile
Hotels in vicinity Glen Eagle and Moat House, Harpenden

HARTLEY WINTNEY (115)

Hartley Wintney, Basingstoke, Hants.
Tel: Basingstoke 2214

Founded 1893 300 members
18 holes 6,004 yards S.S.S. 69 Parkland
Green fees Mon.-Fri. £1.30 per rd. £2 per day
Weekends £2.20 (restricted)
Professional J. Byles
Visiting societies No provision
Meals Not available
Nearest railway station Winchfield 3 miles
Hotels in vicinity Lamb, Hartley Wintney

HASTE HILL (116)

The Drive, Northwood, Middx.
Tel: Northwood 26485

18 holes 5,829 yards S.S.S. 69 Parkland
Green fees Mon.-Fri. 60p
Weekends 85p
Professional J. Priestley
Visiting societies By arrangement with the Treasurer, London Borough of Hillingdon
Meals Light meals and snacks available
Nearest railway station Northwood or Northwood Hills (Metropolitan line tube)
Hotels in vicinity Reindeer and True Lovers Knott, Northwood

HASTINGS (117)

Beauport Park, St Leonard's-on-Sea, Sussex
Tel: Hastings 52977

18 holes 6,325 yards S.S.S. 70 Parkland
Green fees Mon.-Fri. 80p per rd.
Weekends £1.20 per day

Professional J. Grundy
Visiting societies Terms by arrangement
Meals Lunch every day (to be ordered in advance)
Nearest railway station St Leonard's-on-Sea
Hotels in vicinity Beauport Park and High Beech Motel

Pelham Crescent, Hastings

HAWKHURST (118)

High Street, Hawkhurst, Kent
Tel: Hawkhurst 2396

9 holes 4,844 yards S.S.S. 63 Parkland
Green fees Mon.-Fri. £1.25
Weekends £1.75
Visiting societies Weekdays only. Terms by arrangement
Meals Lunch
Nearest railway station
Hotels in vicinity Royal Oak and Tudor Arms, Hawkhurst

HAYLING (119)

Ferry Road, Hayling Island, Hants.
Tel: Hayling Island 4446

18 holes 6,510 yards S.S.S. 71 Seaside links
Green fees Mon.-Fri. £2.50 per day
Weekends £3.50 per day
Professional F. Gilbride
Visiting societies Weekdays only. Terms by arrangement

Meals Lunch every day (to be ordered by 10 a.m.)
Nearest railway station Portsmouth
Hotels in vicinity Sinah Warren Hotel, Newtown

HAYWARDS HEATH (120)

High Beech Lane, Haywards Heath, Sussex
Tel: Lindfield 2157

Founded 1922
18 holes 5,945 yards S.S.S. 68 Undulating parkland
Green fees Mon.-Fri. £2
Sat. £2.16
Sun. £2.70
Professional Bernard Firkins
Membership Waiting list
Visiting societies Max. 40 Weekdays only. £4.50 per head
Meals Lunch (advance notice requested)
Nearest railway station Haywards Heath 2 miles
Hotels in vicinity Hayworthe Arms and Birch, Haywards Heath

HENDON (121)

Off Sanders Lane, London NW7
Tel: 01-346 6023

Founded 1900 400 members
18 holes 6,230 yards S.S.S. 70
Green fees Mon.-Fri. £2.50 (unlimited)
Weekends £4 (by arrangement only)
Professional Stuart Murray
Visiting societies Tues. and Thurs. only. Terms by arrangement
Meals Full catering (except Mon.)
Nearest railway station Mill Hill East ½ mile
Hotels in vicinity Hendon Hall

HENLEY (122)

Harpsden, Henley-on-Thames, Oxon.
Tel: Henley 3304

Founded 1908
18 holes 6,201 yards S.S.S. 70 Hilly parkland

Green fees Mon.-Fri. £3.30 per rd./day
Weekends with member only

Professional D. C. Craik

Visiting societies Max. 40 £5 approx. per head

Meals By prior arrangement with the Steward

Nearest railway station Henley-on-Thames 1 mile

Hotels in vicinity Red Lion and Catherine Wheel, Henley-on-Thames

HERNE BAY (123)

Thanet Way, Herne Bay, Kent

Tel: Herne Bay 3964

18 holes 5,314 yards S.S.S. 66 Parkland

Green fees Mon.-Fri. £1.30
Weekends £1.85

Professional D. Brown

Visiting societies Terms by arrangement

Meals Bar snacks only (except Mon.)

Nearest railway station Herne Bay

HIGHGATE (124)

Denewood Road, Highgate, London N6

Tel: 01-340 3745

18 holes 6,005 yards S.S.S. 70 Parkland

Green fees Mon.-Fri. £2.25 per rd. £3.25 per day
Weekends, visitors not usually accepted

Visiting societies Terms by arrangement

Meals Lunch and tea daily

Nearest railway station Highgate (Northern line tube)

HIGHWOODS (125)

Ellerslie Lane, Bexhill-on-Sea, Sussex TN39 4LJ

Tel: Bexhill 212625

Founded: 1925 630 members

18 holes 6,215 yards S.S.S. 70

Green fees Mon.-Fri. £2 per rd. £2.50 per day
Weekends £2.50 per rd. £3 per day
Sun. with member only
Only bona fide club members with handicap cert.
Advisable to telephone in advance

Professional R. J. McLean

Membership Full subscription £34.50 p.a. (E.F. £40)

Visiting societies Foursomes max. 60, singles max. 30
Terms on application

Meals Bar snacks (except Mon.) and lunch Sat. and Sun.

Nearest railway station Bexhill-on-Sea 3 miles

Hotels in vicinity Whydown and Cooden Beach

HILL BARN (126)

Worthing, Sussex

Tel: Worthing 37301

Venue in the past for Penfold and Martini professional events

18 holes 6,083 yards S.S.S. 69 Downland

Green fees Mon.-Fri. 88p
Weekends £1.15

Professional P. Higgins

Visiting societies Max. 40 Charge as green fees plus catering requirements

Meals Available

Nearest railway station Worthing 1½ miles

Hotels in vicinity Chatsworth and Spaniard, Worthing

HILLINGDON (127)

Dorset Way, Hillingdon, Middx.

Tel: Uxbridge 39810

Founded 1892 250 members

9 holes 5,429 yards S.S.S. 65 Parkland

Green fees Mon.-Fri. £1.50 per rd./day
Weekends with member only

Professional C. A. Price

Membership Full subscription £32 p.a. (E.F. £30)

Visiting societies Not catered for

Meals Bar snacks only

Nearest railway station Uxbridge (Metropolitan and Piccadilly line tube)

Hotels in vicinity London Airport hotels

HINDHEAD (128)

Churt Road, Hindhead, Surrey GU26 6HX

Tel: Hindhead 4614

Founded 1905 550 members

18 holes 6,341 yards S.S.S. 70 Heather and heathland

Green fees Mon.-Fri. £2.20 (£1.20 with member)
Weekends £3.30 (£1.65 with member)

Professional J. A. Little

Membership Full subscription £38.50 (E.F. £38.50)
(£30 compulsory interest free loan)

Visiting societies Max. 40 £5.50 per head

Meals All meals available Wed.-Sun.

Nearest railway station Haslemere 3 miles

Hotels in vicinity Punch, Hindhead; Frensham Pond Hotel, Churt

HOCKLEY (129)

Twyford, Winchester, Hants.

Tel: Twyford 713165

Founded 1915 650 members Unique winter foursomes open to all (inc. profs.)

18 holes 6,135 yards S.S.S. 69

Green fees Mon.-Fri. £2 per rd./day
Weekends with member only

Professional W. G. Matthews

Visiting societies Restricted. Terms by arrangement

Meals By arrangement with the Stewardess

Nearest railway station Winchester 2½ miles

Hotels in vicinity Wessex, Winchester

HOLLINGBURY PARK (130)

Ditchling Road, Brighton, Sussex

Tel: Brighton 552010

Founded 1910 300 members

18 holes 6,399 yards S.S.S. 70 Hilly downland

Green fees Mon.-Fri. £1 per rd. £1.30 per day
Weekends £1.30 per rd.

Professional Peter Brown

Membership Full subscription £7.50 p.a. (E.F. £10)

Visiting societies Green fees plus catering requirements by arrangement

Meals Varied menu available

Nearest railway station Brighton

Hotels in vicinity Royal Pavilion and Clarence, Brighton

HOLTYE (131)

The Club House, Holtye Common, Cowden, Kent
Tel: Cowden 635

Founded Before 1899 In very early days, when there were only 3 holes, nicknamed 'lilliput G.C.'
400 members

9 holes 5,259 yards S.S.S. 66 Heathland

Green fees Mon.-Fri. £1.10 (with member 55p)
Weekends £2.20 (with member £1.65)
No introduction necessary except on Sun. a.m.

Professional Brian Hemsley

Membership Full subscription £23.10 p.a. (E.F. £23.10)

Visiting societies Normal green fees plus catering as required

Meals At White Horse Inn (adjoining Clubhouse), by prior arrangement (tel: Cowden 640)

Nearest railway station Cowden 2 miles

Hotels in vicinity Sussex Oak, Blackham

HOME PARK (132)

Hampton Wick, Kingston-upon-Thames, Surrey
Tel: 01-977 6645

Founded 1895

18 holes 6,437 yards S.S.S. 71 Flat parkland close to the River Thames. Views of Hampton Court Palace

Green fees Mon.-Fri. £1 per rd.
Weekends £1.50 per rd.

Professional Len Roberts

Visiting societies Max. 60 Terms by arrangement

Meals Full catering (except Fri.)

Nearest railway station Hampton Wick 1 mile

Hotels in vicinity Griffin, Kingston-upon-Thames

Hampton Court Palace

HORSENDEN HILL (133)

Woodlands Rise, off Whitton Avenue, Greenford, Middx.

Tel: 01-902 4555

9 holes 6,300 yards S.S.S. 64 Undulating parkland

Green fees 60p

Professional N. McDonald

Visiting societies Not catered for

Meals Light meals and snacks available

Nearest railway station

HUNTERCOMBE (134)

Nuffield, Henley-on-Thames, Oxon.

Tel: Nettlebed 207

Founded 1901 Course designed by Willie Park. Original layout virtually unchanged
430 members

18 holes 6,220 yards S.S.S. 70 Wooded heathland

Green fees Mon.-Fri. £2.75
Sat. £3.30
Sun. £4.40
Introduction preferred

Professional J. B. Draycott

Membership Full subscription £60 p.a. (E.F. £60)

Visiting societies Max. 50 Weekdays only. £5 approx. per head

Meals Lunch and tea every day

Nearest railway station Henley-on-Thames 6 miles

Hotels in vicinity Red Lion and Angel, Henley; White Hart, Nettlebed; Crown, Pishill

HYTHE IMPERIAL (135)

Princes Parade, Hythe, Kent

Tel: Hythe 67441

Founded Pre-war, reformed 1950 300 members

9 holes 5,444 yards S.S.S. 66 Seaside

Green fees Mon.-Fri. £1.50 per rd.
Weekends £2 per rd.

Professional A. A. Mitchell

Visiting societies Not catered for

Meals Full catering at Hotel Imperial, adjoining

Nearest railway station Sandling Junction 3 miles
Folkestone Central 3 miles

Hotels in vicinity Imperial and Stade Court, Hythe

IFIELD (136)

Rusper Road, Ifield, Nr Crawley, Sussex

Tel: Crawley 20222

Founded 1926

18 holes 6,265 yards S.S.S. 70 Downland

Green fees Mon.-Fri. £1.65 per rd.
Weekends £2.20 with member, a.m. only

Professional Barry Blader

Membership Waiting list for male membership
Ladies' subscription £33 p.a. (E.F. £55)

Visiting societies Mon., Tues., Thurs. and Fri. £2.20 (plus service charge)

Meals Full catering service

Nearest railway station Ifield 1 mile

Hotels in vicinity All Gatwick Airport hotels within 4 miles

ILFORD (137)

Wanstead Park Road, Ilford, Essex

Tel: 01-554 2930

18 holes 5,620 yards S.S.S. 67 Parkland

Green fees Mon.-Fri. £1.50
Weekends £2.25 (plus VAT)
Visitors restricted at weekends. Prior booking advisable

Professional A. Campbell

Visiting societies Weekdays only Terms on application

Meals Lunch every day (except Mon.)

Nearest railway station Ilford

JOHN O' GAUNT (138)

Sutton Park, Sandy, Beds.

Tel: Potton 260252

Founded 1948

18 holes 6,365 yards S.S.S. 71

9 holes 3,208 yards S.S.S. 36 Parkland and sand

Green fees Mon.-Fri. £1.70
Weekends £3.35

Professional M. F. Foster

Membership Waiting list

Visiting societies Max. 110 according to catering requirements

Meals Always available

Nearest railway station Biggleswade 3 miles

Hotels in vicinity Rose & Crown, Potton; Crown Hotel, Biggleswade

KINGSTHORPE (139)

Kingsley Road, Northampton, Northants.

Tel: Northampton 31142

18 holes 5,880 yards S.S.S. 68 Parkland

Green fees Mon.-Fri. £1.65 per day
Weekends with member only

Professional J. Freeman

Visiting societies By arrangement

Meals Lunch and tea (prior notice requested)

Nearest railway station Northampton

Hotels in vicinity Saxon Inn Motel and Grand, Northampton

KINGSWOOD (140)

Kingswood, Tadworth, Surrey

Tel: Mogador 2188

18 holes 6,445 yards S.S.S. 71 Parkland

Green fees Mon.-Fri. £1.50 per rd. £2.25 per day
Weekends £3.50 per rd./day
Bona fide club members only

Professional K. Macpherson

Visiting societies Terms on application

Meals Lunch daily

Nearest railway station Tadworth

KNEBWORTH (141)

Deard's End Lane, Knebworth, Herts. SG3 6NL

Tel: Knebworth 2752

18 holes 6,440 yards S.S.S. 71

Green fees Mon.-Fri. £2 per rd. £3 per day
Weekends with member only

Professional A. Hull

Visiting societies Mon., Tues. and Thurs. only Terms by arrangement

Meals Lunch and dinner daily (prior booking requested)

Nearest railway station Knebworth

Hotels in vicinity Roebuck Motel and Grampian, Knebworth

KNOLE PARK (142)

Seal Hollow Road, Sevenoaks, Kent

Tel: Sevenoaks 52150

Founded 1924 600 members

18 holes 6,249 yards S.S.S. 70 Parkland

Green fees Mon.-Fri. £2 per rd. £3 per day
Prior confirmation by telephone advisable
Weekends with member only
Public hols. with member only

Professional S. L. King

Membership Membership list closed

Visiting societies Max. 32 £5.50 per day inc.

Meals Lunch, tea and snacks

Nearest railway station Sevenoaks 1 mile

Hotels in vicinity Any hotel in Sevenoaks convenient

LALEHAM (143)

Laleham Reach, Mixnams Lane, Chertsey, Surrey

Tel: Chertsey 64211

Founded 1907 480 members

18 holes 6,093 yards S.S.S. 69 Flat parkland course on island in the River Thames

Green fees Mon.-Fri. £1.65 per rd. £2 per day
Sat. £2.75 per rd./day
Sun. with member only

Professional G. Webb
(A. Grubb, D. Nankerville and K. Benson—Tournament players)

Membership Membership lists closed

Visiting societies Average two societies per week. £3.85 fully inc.

Meals All available every day

Nearest railway station Chertsey or Staines 3 miles

Hotels in vicinity Packhorse, Staines

LAMBERHURST (144)

Church Road, Lamberhurst, Kent

Tel: Lamberhurst 241

9 holes 5,336 yards S.S.S. 65 Parkland
Tee variations on second nine

Green fees Mon.-Fri. £1.25 per rd./day
Weekends £1.80
Reduction with member

Professional C. Millyard

Visiting societies Small groups only. Terms by arrangement

Meals Light lunch (except Fri.)

Nearest railway station Frant (nr. Tunbridge Wells)

Hotels in vicinity Horse & Groom, Lamberhurst

LANGLEY PARK (145)

Barnfield Wood Road, Beckenham, Kent

Tel: 01-658 6849

Founded 1913 650 members

18 holes 6,534 yards S.S.S. 71 Parkland, well-wooded

Green fees Mon.-Fri. £2.75 per rd. £4 per day
No visitors weekends or Public hols.
Introduction necessary
Advised to telephone prior to visit

Professional W. Hitchcock

Membership Full subscription £60 p.a. (E.F. £90)

Visiting societies Max. 40 Wed. only. £6.50 per head

Meals Lunch and tea

Nearest railway station Bromley South 1½ miles

Hotels in vicinity Bromley Court, Bromley

LEATHERHEAD (146)

Oxshott Road, Leatherhead, Surrey

Tel: Leatherhead 74348

Founded 1903 550 members

18 holes 6,238 yards S.S.S. 70 Heathland

Green fees Mon.-Fri. £1.65
Weekends £3.30
Introduction required

Professional R. Richards

Membership Lists closed

Visiting societies Max. 30-40 Charges by arrangement

Meals All meals every day until 6.30 p.m. (later by arrangement with the Steward)

Nearest railway station Leatherhead 2½ miles

Hotels in vicinity New Bull, Leatherhead

LEIGHTON BUZZARD (147)

Plantation Road, Leighton Buzzard, Beds.

Tel: Leighton Buzzard 3188

Founded 1925 240 members

10 holes (2nd and 11th diff.) 6,014 yards S.S.S. 69

Green fees Mon.-Fri. £1.50 per day (£1 with member)
Weekends £2 with member only
Public hols. £2 with member only

Professional Stephen Hann

Membership Full subscription £25 p.a. (E.F. £35)
(Special terms: over 65s, husband & wife)

Visiting societies Max. 30 £5 per head

Meals Available every day (except Mon.)

Nearest railway station Leighton Buzzard 1½ miles

Hotels in vicinity Hunt, Leighton Buzzard; Village Green Motel, Northall

LETCHWORTH (148)

Letchworth Lane, Letchworth, Herts.

Tel: Letchworth 3203

Founded 1907

18 holes 6,010 yards S.S.S. 69 Parkland, plenty of trees

Green fees Mon.-Fri. £1.60 per rd. £2.20 per day
Weekends with member only
Introduction necessary

Professional S. J. Mutimer

Membership All waiting lists closed

Visiting societies Max. 50 Fees in accordance with catering required

Meals Every day (except Mon.)

Nearest railway station Hitchin 2 miles, Letchworth 1 mile

Hotels in vicinity Letchworth Hall (adjacent)

LEWES (149)

Chapel Hill, Lewes, Sussex

Tel: Lewes 3245

Founded 1896 330 members

18 holes 5,670 yards S.S.S. 67 Downland

Green fees Mon.-Fri. £1.25 per day
Weekends £1.75 per day
Public hols. £1.75 per day

Professional E. F. Goldring

Membership Full subscription £30 p.a. (E.F. £30)

Visiting societies Max. 40 Approx. £5 per head

Meals 24 hours' notice required

Nearest railway station Lewes ½ mile

Hotels in vicinity Shelleys and White Hart, Lewes

LIPHOOK (150)

Liphook, Hants.

Tel: Liphook 723271

Founded 1922 880 members

18 holes 6,256 yards S.S.S. 70 Sandy but heather-clad, with bracken and fir trees; a natural course

Green fees Mon.-Fri. £2.20
Weekends £2.75
Introduction necessary

Professional I. Large

Membership Full subscription £35 p.a. (E.F. £35)
Waiting lists for all categories

Visiting societies Only those already established with club may reapply

Meals Lunch, light tea and snacks at bar

Nearest railway station Liphook 4 miles. Taxi essential, club situated 1 mile up private road off the A3

Hotels in vicinity Royal Anchor and Post, Liphook

LITTLEHAMPTON (151)

Riverside West, Littlehampton, Sussex

Tel: Littlehampton 7170

18 holes 6,072 yards S.S.S. 69 Seaside

Green fees Mon.-Fri. £2
Weekends £2.75
Reductions when playing with member

Professional N. Greer

Visiting societies Wed. and Fri. only. Terms by arrangement

Meals Lunch available Wed. inc.

Nearest railway station Littlehampton

Hotels in vicinity Beach, Littlehampton; Birer's, Climping

LITTLESTONE (152)

St Andrews Road, Littlestone, New Romney, Kent

Tel: New Romney 3355

Founded 1888 400 members

18 holes 6,453 yards S.S.S. 71 Seaside links
(Short 9 holes also available, 2,115 yards, par 32)

Green fees On application to the Secretary

Professional G. Williams

Visiting societies Max. 60 Weekdays only
Charges by arrangement

Meals All available (except Tues.)

Nearest railway station Ashford, Kent 15 miles

Hotels in vicinity Dormy House and Windacre, Littlestone;
Broadacres, Ship and New Inn, New Romney

LONDON SCOTTISH (153)

Windmill Enclosure, Wimbledon Common, Surrey

Tel: 01-789 7517

Founded 1865 Oldest club in England and Wales playing on its original course
250 members (men only)

18 holes 5,435 yards S.S.S. 66 Well-wooded common land with no bunkers

Green fees Mon.-Fri. 85p
Weekends £1.10 with member only
Players must wear red

Professional W. S. Attwood

Membership Full subscription £28 p.a. (E.F. £10 plus VAT)

Visiting societies By arrangement

Meals Meals and snacks (except Mon.)

Nearest railway station Wimbledon (District line tube) 2 miles

Hotels in vicinity Dog & Fox, Wimbledon Hill

LULLINGSTONE PARK (154)

Lullingstone Park, Park Gate, Chelsfield, Orpington, Kent

Tel: Badgers Mount 517

18 holes 6,626 yards S.S.S. 72 Parkland

Green fees Mon.-Fri. 60p
Weekends 80p
Municipal course, no introduction necessary

Professional G. Lloyd

Visiting societies Not catered for at present

Meals Lunch daily (to be ordered in advance)

Nearest railway station Orpington

Hotels in vicinity Bull, Swanley; Lion, Farningham

MAIDENHEAD (155)

Shoppenhangers Road, Maidenhead, Berks.

Tel: Maidenhead 24693

Founded 1898 500 members

18 holes 6,500 yards S.S.S. 70 Parkland

Green fees Mon.-Fri. £2.75 per rd.
Weekends no visitors
Introduction necessary

Professional R. Newman

Visiting societies Small groups preferred. £5 per head, inc.

Meals Available

Nearest railway station Maidenhead 200 yards

Hotels in vicinity Esso Motor, Maidenhead

MALDEN (156)

Traps Lane, New Malden, Surrey

Tel: 01-942 0654

Founded 1894 600 members

18 holes 6,314 yards S.S.S. 70 Well-wooded parkland

Green fees Mon.-Fri. £2
Weekends £4
(Playing with member £1.50)

Professional G. Howard

Membership Full subscription £60 p.a. (E.F. £60)

Visiting societies £5 per head (plus VAT)

Meals All meals available every day

Nearest railway station New Malden ½ mile
Hotels in vicinity Griffin, Kingston-upon-Thames

MALDON (157)

Beeleigh, Langford, Maldon, Essex
Tel: Maldon 53212

Founded 1891 325 members
9 holes 6,077 yards S.S.S. 69
Green fees Mon.-Fri. £1 per rd.
Sat. £1.50
Sun. with member only
Any day with member 75p
Professional F. G. Smith
Membership Full subscription £25 p.a. (E.F. £25)
Visiting societies No provision
Meals Not available
Nearest railway station Witham 4 miles
Hotels in vicinity Blue Boar and King's Head, Maldon

MANNINGS HEATH (158)

Golding Lane, Mannings Heath, Nr Horsham, Sussex
Tel: Horsham 5224

Founded 1919 700 members
18 holes 6,300 yards S.S.S. 70
Green fees Mon.-Fri. £2
Weekends £2.75
Public hols. £2.75
Only bona fide golfers with handicaps under 18
Professional Paul Huggett
Membership Full subscription £33 p.a. (E.F. £30)
Visiting societies Weekdays only. Advisable to book well in advance. Approx. £4.50 per head all inc.
Meals Lunch and dinner by prior arrangement (except Tues.)
Nearest railway station Horsham 3 miles
Hotels King's Head, Horsham

MAYLANDS (159)

Colchester Road, Romford, Essex

Tel: Ingrebourne 42055

Founded 1936 700 members

18 holes 6,101 yards S.S.S. 69 Undulating parkland

Green fees On application to the Secretary
Bona fide club members only

Professional Roger Willy

Visiting societies Weekdays only. Terms by arrangement

Meals Full restaurant

Nearest railway station Harold Wood 2 miles

Hotels in vicinity Moat House, Brentwood

MID HERTS (160)

Gustard Wood, Wheathampstead, Herts.

Tel: Wheathampstead 3118

18 holes 6,100 yards S.S.S. 70 Parkland and common land

Green fees All enquiries to Secretary
Weekends with member only

Professional M. Steadman

Visiting societies Weekdays only Terms by arrangement

Meals Lunch daily

Nearest railway station Wheathampstead

Hotels in vicinity Bull, Wheathampstead

MID KENT (161)

Singlewood Road, Gravesend, Kent

Tel: Gravesend 68035

550 members

18 holes 6,053 yards S.S.S. 69 Parkland

Green fees Mon.-Fri. £2.20 (£1.10 with member)
Weekends £2.75 (£1.38 with member)
Certified handicap necessary

Professional K. Airth

Membership Full subscription £32 (E.F. £40)

Visiting societies On application

Meals As required on application

Nearest railway station Gravesend 2½ miles

Hotels in vicinity Clarendon Royal, Woodlands and Laughing Water Motel, Gravesend

MILL HILL (162)

100 Barnet Way, Mill Hill, London NW7

Tel: 01-959 2339

18 holes 6,418 yards S.S.S. 71 Parkland

Green fees On application to the Secretary

Professional A. Daniel

Visiting societies Terms by arrangement

Meals Lunch daily

Nearest railway station Mill Hill East (Northern line tube)

Hotels in vicinity Brent Bridge, Brent; Hendon Hall, Hendon

MITCHAM (163)

Mitcham Junction, Surrey

Tel: 01-648 1508

18 holes 5,898 yards S.S.S. 68 Common land

Green fees Mon.-Fri. 50p per rd. 75p per day
Weekends 75p per rd. £1.10 per day
Restricted weekends

Professional J. A. Godfrey

Visiting societies Not usually catered for

Meals Light snacks

Nearest railway station Mitcham Junction

MOOR PARK (164)

Moor Park, Rickmansworth, Herts. WD3 1QN

Tel: Rickmansworth 73146

Founded 1924 Courses built on land containing prehistoric and Roman remains
Clubhouse also of historical interest. Venue for many top professional and amateur tournaments

36 holes High course: 6,695 yards S.S.S. 72
West course: 5,823 yards S.S.S. 68
Undulating parkland, well-wooded

Green fees Mon.-Fri. £4 per day
Weekends no visitors

Professional Ross Whitehead

Visiting societies Max. 60 (one course only) £6 per head inc.

Meals Lunch and tea à la carte

Nearest railway station Moor Park (Metropolitan line tube) 1 mile

Hotels in vicinity Bedford Arms, Chenies; Victoria, Rickmansworth

MUSWELL HILL (165)

Rhodes Avenue, Wood Green, London N22

Tel: 01-888 1764

18 holes 6,446 yards S.S.S. 71 Parkland

Green fees Mon.-Fri. £2.35 per rd./day
Weekends £1.15 with member only

Professional J. Hamilton

Visiting societies Terms on application

Meals Light meals available

Nearest railway station Wood Green (Piccadilly line tube)

NEVILL (166)

Benhall Mill Road, Tunbridge Wells, Kent

Tel: Tunbridge Wells 25818

Founded 1915 Original 9 holes laid out by James Braid. A further 9 added in 1920. In 1966 course was redesigned and reconstructed under the supervision of Henry Cotton
600 members

18 holes 6,336 yards S.S.S. 70 Wooded countryside with heather and gorse

Green fees Mon.-Fri. £2 per rd. £2.50 per day
Weekends £3 per rd. £4 per day
Bona fide club members only, with handicap cert.

Professional N. Huckell

Membership Full subscription £43.50 (E.F. £55)

Visiting societies Max. 64 Weekdays only. £3 per head
Catering by arrangement

Meals Available (except Mon.)
Visitors required to book in advance

Nearest railway station Tunbridge Wells Central 1 mile

Hotels in vicinity Calverley and Wellington, Tunbridge Wells

NEW ZEALAND (167)

Woodham Lane, Woodham, Weybridge, Surrey KT14 3QD

Tel: Byfleet 45049

Founded 1895 300 members

18 holes 6,012 yards S.S.S. 69 Heathland, sandy soil

Green fees Mon.-Fri. with member £1.10
introduced by member £1.65
with introduction at Secretary's discretion £2.75

Weekends with member £1.65
introduced by member £2.20

Professional J. Clements

Membership Full subscription £50 p.a. (E.F. £50)

Visiting societies Max. 50 Tues. & Fri. only. £6 per head

Meals Lunch and tea (except Thurs.)

Nearest railway station West Byfleet ½ mile

Hotels in vicinity Ship, Weybridge

NEWBURY & CROOKHAM (168)

Bury's Bank Road, Greenham, Newbury, Berks. RG15 8BZ

Tel: Newbury 35

Founded 1873 590 members
Venue for summer pro/am tournaments

18 holes 5,843 yards S.S.S. 68 Undulating with magnificent views over Newbury Racecourse and the Kennet Valley

Green fees Mon.-Fri. £1.50 per rd. £2.20 per day
Weekends £3.30 per rd./£4.40 per day
Visitors welcome with reservation only

Professional J. S. Hughes

Membership Full subscription £35 p.a. (E.F. £35)

Visiting societies Green fee plus 25p per head for grats.

Meals Lunch and tea daily except Thurs.
Thurs.—bar snacks only

Nearest railway station Newbury 2½ miles

Hotels in vicinity Chequers and Broadway, Newbury

NEWTON GREEN (169)

Newton, Sudbury, Suffolk

Tel: Sudbury 2535

9 holes 5,400 yards S.S.S. 65 Moorland common

Green fees On application. Visitors welcome all week and after 12 noon on Sun.

Professional A. Davey

Visiting Societies Not catered for

Meals Lunch served at Inn adjoining course

Nearest railway station Sudbury

Hotels in vicinity Saracen's Head Inn, Newton

NORTH DOWNS (170)

Northdown Road, Woldingham, Caterham, Surrey
Tel: Woldingham 3298

Founded 1899 Extended to 18 holes in 1971
750 members

18 holes 6,054 yards S.S.S. 69 Downland

Green fees Mon.-Fri. £1.50
Weekends with member only

Professional A. T. Bennett

Membership Full subscription £40 p.a. (E.F. £40)

Visiting societies Max. 24 £2.50 green fee plus cost of meals

Meals Available every day (except Mon.), prior notice necessary

Nearest railway station Woldingham 2 miles

Hotels in vicinity In Caterham or Oxted, Surrey

NORTH FORELAND (171)

Convent Road, Broadstairs, Kent
Tel: Thanet 62140

Founded 1903 Then called Kingsgate G.C., with only 9 holes. 1909 Lord Northcliffe bought it and extended it to full 18 holes. Name was changed to North Foreland
850 members

18 holes 6,278 yards S.S.S. 70 Coastal
Pitch and putt course, par 54, 1,752 yards

Green fees Mon.-Fri. £2 Pitch and putt 50p
Weekends £3 Pitch and putt £1

Professional D. Bonthron

Membership Full subscription £42.90

Visiting societies Small parties, Tues., Wed. and Thurs. only. Charges on application

Meals All meals available

Nearest railway station Broadstairs 1½ miles

Hotels in vicinity Castle Keep and Fayreness, Broadstairs

NORTH HANTS (172)

Minley Road, Fleet, Hants.
Tel: Fleet 6443

Founded 1904 650 members Venue for several top amateur Open events

18 holes 6,231 yards S.S.S. 70 Heathland with pine trees

Green fees Mon.-Fri. £2.75
Weekends £4.50
Introduction necessary

Professional R. E. Mounce

Membership Full subscription £40 p.a. (E.F. £50)
Waiting lists for all categories

Visiting societies Max. 40 £3.30 per head per day

Meals Lunch and high tea daily (except Mon.)

Nearest railway station Fleet 400 yards

Hotels in vicinity Lismoyne, Beacon and Station, Fleet

NORTH MIDDLESEX (173)

Friern Barnet Lane, Whetstone, London N20

Tel: 01-445 1604

18 holes 5,620 yards S.S.S. 67 Parkland

Green fees Mon.-Fri. £1.85 per rd. £2.20 per day
Weekends £1.25 with member only

Professional A. Horsman

Visiting societies One month's notice required

Meals Lunch daily (except Mon.)

Nearest railway station Totteridge & Whetstone (Northern line tube)

Radcliffe Camera : Oxford.

NORTH OXFORD (174)

Banbury Road, Oxford

Tel: Oxford 54924

Founded 1907

18 holes 5,824 yards S.S.S. 67 Parkland

Green fees Mon.-Fri. £1.75
Weekends £3.50
Reduction with member

Professional P. Lester

Visiting societies Terms by arrangement

Meals Catering available

Nearest railway station Oxford

Hotels in vicinity Watney Lyons Motel and Royal Oxford, Oxford

NORTHAMPTON (175)

Kettering Road, Northampton, Northants.

Tel: Northampton 33511

18 holes 6,007 yards S.S.S. 69 Parkland

Green fees Mon.-Fri. £1.25 per rd./day
Weekends £1.75 with member only

Professional A. Lovelady

Visiting societies Terms by arrangement

Meals Lunch daily (except Tues.), to be ordered in advance

Nearest railway station Northampton

Hotels in vicinity Westone, Grand and Saxon Inn, Northampton

NORTHAMPTONSHIRE (176)

Church Brampton, Northampton, Northants.

Tel: Northampton 842170

Founded 1910 775 members Popular venue for top amateur events in Midlands

18 holes 6,397 yards S.S.S. 70 Heathland

Green fees Mon.-Fri. £2 per day
Weekends £2.50 per day

Professional E. Overend

Visiting societies Weekdays only (main society day Wed.). Green fees plus meals

Meals Full menu available, bar snacks only Fri.

Nearest railway station Northampton 4½ miles

Hotels in vicinity Saxon Inn and Westone, Northampton; Albany Motor, Crick

NORTHWOOD (177)

Rickmansworth Road, Northwood, Middx.

Tel: Northwood 21384

Founded 1891 600 members

18 holes 6,495 yards S.S.S. 71 Parkland

Green fees Mon.-Fri. £2.20 per rd.
Weekends with members only

Professional P. Cafferty

Membership Full subscription £60 p.a. (E.F. £60)

Visiting societies Weekdays only. £2 per rd. plus catering requirements

Meals Catering available

Nearest railway station Northwood (Metropolitan line tube) 10 minutes

Hotels in vicinity Several in Watford and Harrow

OLD FOLD MANOR (178)

Hadley Green, Barnet, Herts.

Tel: 01-449 2266

Founded 1910

18 holes 6,473 yards S.S.S. 71 Sandy sub-soil, dry

Green fees Mon.-Fri. £1.65 per day
Weekends £3.30 (restricted)

Professional P. Jones

Membership Full subscription £48 p.a. (E.F. £36)

Visiting societies Max. 40 Thurs. and Fri. only. £4.95 per head

Meals Full catering (except Mon. and Wed.)

Nearest railway station Barnet (Northern line tube) ½ mile

ORSETT (179)

Brentwood Road, Orsett, Essex

Tel: Grays Thurrock 891352

Founded 1902 Redesigned 1930 850 members

18 holes 6,619 yards S.S.S. 72 Heathland

Green fees £2.20 per rd. £3.30 per day
Must be a member of a club

Professional Gordon Roberts

Membership Subscription £50 p.a. (E.F. £50)

Visiting societies Max. 40 £3.30-£6 per head
Meals Every day (except Fri.)
Nearest railway station Grays or Stanford-le-Hope
Hotels in vicinity Fairlane Motel, Upminster

PEACEHAVEN (180)

Brighton Road, Newhaven, Sussex BN9 9UH
Tel: Newhaven 4049

Founded 1899 Reopened 1923 275 members
18 holes 5,473 yards S.S.S. 67 Downland
Green fees Mon.-Fri. £1.10 (with member 82½p)
Weekends £2.20 (with member £1.10)
Handicap cert. required
Professional Colin Diplock
Membership Full subscription £22 p.a. (E.F. £20)
Visiting societies Not catered for
Meals Available with advance notice
Nearest railway station Newhaven Town 2 miles
Hotels in vicinity Peacehaven; Mercury Motel, Seaford

PERIVALE PARK (181)

Lever Gardens, Western Avenue, Greenford, Middx.
Tel: 01-578 1693

Founded 1930 200 members
9 holes 5,260 yards S.S.S. 65
Green fees Mon.-Fri. 22p
Weekends 27p
Season tickets available
Municipal course, introduction not necessary
Professional K. Moss
Visiting societies Not catered for
Meals Bar snacks and light refreshments only
Nearest railway station Perivale (Central line tube) 10 minutes
Hotels in vicinity Myllet Arms, Greenford

PETERSFIELD (182)

Petersfield, Hants.
Tel: Petersfield 3725

Founded 1890 350 members

9 holes 5,666 yards S.S.S. 67 Dry and sandy

Green fees Mon.-Fri. £1 per rd.
Weekends £1.50 per rd.

Professional R. L. Roberts

Visiting societies No provision

Meals Not available

Nearest railway station Petersfield ½ mile

Hotels in vicinity Red Lion, Drum and Railway Arms

Uppark

PILTDOWN (183)

Uckfield, Sussex

Tel: Newick 2033

Founded 1904 350 members

18 holes 6,100 yards S.S.S. 69 Heathland with heather and gorse

Green fees Mon.-Fri. £2 per rd. £2.50 per day
Weekends £2.50 per rd. £3 per day
Sun. after 1 p.m.
Bona fide club members only

Professional John Amos

Membership Full subscription £30 p.a. (E.F. £45)

Visiting societies Max. 36 Mon.-Fri. £4 per head all inc.
Sat. £5 per head all inc.

Meals Lunch (24 hours' notice required)

Nearest railway station Haywards Heath

Hotels in vicinity Maiden's Head, Uckfield

PINNER HILL (184)

Southview Road, Pinner, Middx.

Tel: 01-866 0963

Founded 1927 500 members

18 holes 6,293 yards S.S.S. 70 Hilly woodland

Green fees On application to Secretary

Professional D. Nash

Visiting societies Weekdays only. Terms by arrangement

Meals Available (prior booking requested)

Nearest railway station Northwood Hills (Metropolitan line tube) 1½ miles

PORTERS PARK (185)

Shenley Hill, Radlett, Herts.

Tel: Radlett 6262

Founded 1899

18 holes 6,298 yards S.S.S. 70 Parkland

Green fees Mon.-Fri. £2.20 per rd. £2.75 per day
Weekends introduced by and playing with member only

Professional J. K. Ramsden

Membership Waiting list

Visiting societies Wed. and Thurs. only. £5.50 per head

Meals Daily (except Mon.) by arrangement with the Steward

Nearest railway station Radlett ½ mile

Hotels in vicinity Red Lion, Radlett; Sopwell House, St Albans

PORTSMOUTH (186)

Crookhorn Lane, Widley, Hants.

Tel: Portsmouth 64549

18 holes 5,950 yards S.S.S. 69 Parkland

Green fees Mon.-Fri. 50p. per rd. £1 per day
Weekends 75p per rd. £1.50 per day
No introduction necessary Public course

Professional W. McHardy

Visiting societies No provision

Meals Light refreshments only

Nearest railway station Portsmouth

POTTERS BAR (187)

Darkes Lane, Potters Bar, Herts.

Tel: Potters Bar 52020

Founded 1923 600 members Home club of former Open Champion Tony Jacklin

18 holes 6,217 yards S.S.S. 70 Heathland

Green fees With member only
Mon.-Fri. £2.20
Weekends £3.30

Professional W. Large

Visiting societies Not catered for

Meals Lunch and tea

Nearest railway station Potters Bar ½ mile

PRINCE'S (188)

Sandwich Bay, Kent

Tel: Sandwich 2000

Founded 1904 A very famous links venue: British Open Championship in 1932, and since then several professional tournaments, Schweppes, Piccadilly, Double Diamond

27 holes 6,814 yards S.S.S. 73
(7,145 yards champs. tees)
Sandy loam, flat and undulating
9-hole course 6,440 yards S.S.S. 70

Green fees Mon.-Fri. £2 per rd./day
Weekends £3.50 per rd./day

Professional M. Youngs (tel: Sandwich 3797)

Membership Full subscription £60 p.a. (living within 25 mile radius); £36 p.a. (living within 25-50 mile radius) (E.F. in all categories, £30)

Visiting societies Mon.-Fri. £4 per head (coffee, lunch and tea, inc. service)
Weekends approx. £5.50 per head inc.

Meals Full catering (except Mon.)

Nearest railway station Sandwich 2½ miles

Hotels in vicinity Dormy House and Bell, Sandwich

PURLEY DOWNS (189)

106 Purley Downs Road, Purley, Surrey

Tel: 01-657 8347

Founded 1894

18 holes 6,237 yards S.S.S. 70 Downland

Green fees Mon.-Fri. £3.50 per rd./day
Weekends no visitors
Introduction necessary

Professional G. Wilson

Visiting societies Terms by arrangement

Meals Full catering, prior booking advisable

Nearest railway station Purley Oaks ½ mile, Sanderstead ½ mile

PUTTENHAM (190)

Puttenham, Guildford, Surrey GU3 1AL

Tel: Guildford 810498

Founded 1894 450 members
Original 9 holes redesigned and enlarged to 18 holes in 1937

18 holes 5,339 yards S.S.S. 66 Heathland
One of the driest courses in area

Green fees Mon.-Fri. £2 per rd./day
Weekends £3 per rd./day
Introduction not essential but helpful

Professional R. Donald

Membership Full subscription £25 p.a. (E.F. £25)

Visiting societies Full day £3.50 per head, half day £2
Numbers by arrangement

Meals Available by arrangement with the Steward

Nearest railway station Guildford 4½ miles, Farnham 6 miles

Hotels in vicinity Bush, Farnham; Angel, Guildford

PYECOMBE (191)

Clayton Hill, Pyecombe, Brighton, Sussex BN4 7FF

Tel: Hassocks 4176

Founded 1894 500 members

18 holes 5,655 yards S.S.S. 67 Downland

Green fees Mon.-Fri. £1.50 per day
Weekends £2.20 per day

Professional C. R. White

Membership Full subscription £28 p.a. (E.F. £40)

Visiting societies £1.50 green fee, lunch by arrangement

Meals Lunch and tea to order (except Sun.)

Nearest railway station Hassocks 3 miles

Hotels in vicinity Station, Hassocks

READING (192)

Kidmore End Road, Emmer Green, Reading, Berks.

Tel: Reading 472909

Founded 1910 570 members

18 holes 6,170 yards S.S.S. 69 Undulating parkland, dry winter course

Green fees Mon.-Fri. £2.20 per rd./day (£1.40 with member)
Weekends no visitors

Professional John Larrad

Membership Full subscription £40 p.a. (E.F. £40)

Visiting societies Max. 60 £4-£5 per day

Meals Lunch and dinner on request (except Mon.)

Nearest railway station Reading $2\frac{1}{4}$ miles

Hotels in vicinity Caversham Bridge, Reading

REDHILL & REIGATE (193)

Common Road, Redhill, Surrey

Tel: Redhill 61255

18 holes 5,360 yards S.S.S. 66 Moorland

Green fees Mon.-Fri. 90p per rd. £1.30 per day
Sat. £1.60 per day
Sun. £2.20 per day

Professional M. Hawkins

Meals Lunch daily

Nearest railway station Redhill

Hotels in vicinity Lakers, Reigate

REIGATE HEATH (194)

Reigate Heath, Reigate, Surrey

Tel: Reigate 42610

Founded 1895

9 holes 5,447 yards S.S.S. 66 Heathland

Green fees Mon.-Fri. £1.65 per rd. £2.20 per day
Weekends £2.20 per rd. £2.75 per day
Sun. with member only

Professional W. H. Carter

Visiting societies Max. 32 Wed. & Thurs. only. Green fees plus catering as required

Meals Light lunch and snacks every day (except Fri.) Special requirements by prior order

Nearest railway station Reigate 1 mile

Hotels in vicinity Bridge House and Cranleigh, Reigate

RICHMOND (195)

Sudbrook Park, Richmond, Surrey

Tel: 01-940 1463

Founded 1891 The clubhouse is a Georgian mansion built by James Gibbs in 1726 for the Duke of Argyll. Its main feature is the fine pillared porticos on both facades of the Cube room, now the club's dining room

18 holes 6,060 yards S.S.S. 69 Heavily wooded parkland The course has 6 par 3's

Green fees Mon.-Fri. £3 per rd.
Weekends £4 per rd. (by prior arrangement only)
Visitors must be bona fide club members

Professional Bill Evans

Membership Prospective members must have been known for some years by two sponsors from the club.

Visiting societies Tues. and Thurs. only. Terms on application

Meals Lunch daily (except Mon.), bar snacks and tea every day

Nearest railway station Richmond (main line and District line tube)

Hotels in vicinity Richmond Hill

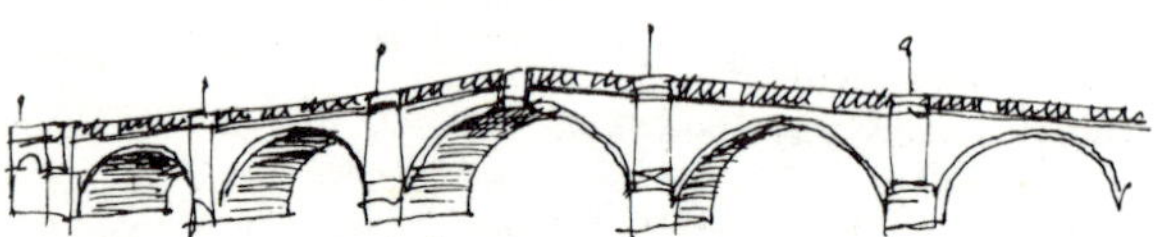

Richmond Bridge

RICKMANSWORTH (196)

Moor Lane, Rickmansworth, Herts.

Tel: Rickmansworth 73163

18 holes 4,551 yards S.S.S. 62 Parkland

Green fees Mon.-Fri. 60p
Weekends £1.10

Professional A. Herd

Visiting societies By prior arrangement with the Treasurer, Rickmansworth Urban District Council

Meals Lunch and tea (except Tues.—light snacks only)

Nearest railway station Rickmansworth (Metropolitan line tube)

Hotels in vicinity Victoria, Rickmansworth

ROCHESTER & COBHAM PARK (197)

Park Pale, By Rochester, Kent ME2 3UD

Tel: Shorne 3411

Founded 1891 600 members

18 holes 6,355 yards S.S.S. 70 Undulating parkland

Green fees Mon.-Fri. £2.20 per rd. £3.30 per day
Weekends with member only
Introduction not essential but desirable

Professional Matt Henderson

Membership Full subscription £50 (E.F. £50)

Visiting societies Max. 40 £5.50-£6 per head according to menu selected

Meals Full menu available (prior booking requested for dinner)

Nearest railway station Gravesend or Strood 5 miles

Hotels in vicinity Laughing Water Inn, Shorne 1 mile

ROCHFORD HUNDRED (198)

Hall Road, Rochford, Essex

Tel: Southend-on-Sea 544302

Founded 1893 The original Southend G.C. moved to Rochford in 1896. Another 9 holes added year later. Course remodelled by James Braid in 1924. 'Hundred' is derived from an ancient territorial division that once occupied the site

18 holes 6,255 yards S.S.S. 70 Flat, constructed round the village church

Green fees Mon.-Fri. £2 per rd. £2.50 per day
Weekends with member only
Introduction necessary from bona fide club members

Professional R. Steel

Membership Full subscription £50 p.a. (E.F. £50)
Waiting list

Visiting societies Max. 24-30 Mon.-Fri. Meals on application

Meals Available any weekday except Mon.

Nearest railway station Rochford ¼ mile

Hotels in vicinity Airport, Southend-on-Sea

Comments Tues.—Ladies' Day
No visitors before 12 noon

Chiswick House

ROEHAMPTON (199)

Roehampton Lane, London SW15

Tel: 01-876 5505

Founded 1902 3,000 members
A sports club with 27 tennis courts (lawn and hard), croquet lawns and swimming pool

18 holes 6,057 yards S.S.S. 69 Parkland, sandy loam

Green fees Mon.-Fri. £1
Weeeknds £2
Visitors must be introduced by and play with member

Professional S. S. Scott

Membership Full subscription £65 (E.F. £60)

Visiting societies No new societies accepted

Meals Lunch and tea daily

Nearest railway station Barnes 300 yards

ROMFORD (200)

Heath Drive, Gidea Park, Essex

Tel: Romford 40986

Founded 1894 Founded by the Members of Whitehall Club, London

18 holes 6,378 yards S.S.S. 72 Parkland

Green fees Mon.-Fri. £2.20 per rd. £3.30 per day
Weekends no visitors
Must be bona fide club members

Professional Harry Flatman

Membership Closed

Visiting societies Max. 40 unless by special arrangement
Tues. and Thurs. only
Charges as per green fees + catering requirements

Meals All meals except on Mon. (lunch to be ordered before 10 a.m.)

Nearest railway station Gidea Park ½ mile

Hotels in vicinity Fairlane Motor Inn, Hornchurch

ROWLAND'S CASTLE (201)

Links Lane, Rowland's Castle, Hampshire

Tel: Rowland's Castle 2784

Founded 1902 545 members

18 holes 6,750 yards S.S.S. 72 Parkland

Green fees On application

Professional P. Roberts

Visiting societies Apply to the Secretary

Meals Lunch and tea daily

Nearest railway station Rowland's Castle ½ mile

Hotels in vicinity Havant Albany Inn, Hayling Island

ROYAL ASHDOWN FOREST (202)

Forest Row, Sussex

Tel: Forest Row 2018

Two 18-hole forest land courses

OLD COURSE

Founded 1888 6,515 yards S.S.S. 71

Members' club Closed Visitors wishing to play over this course should make application to the Secretary

NEW COURSE

Ashdown Forest Hotel

Tel: Forest Row 2010 (Manager's Office)

Founded 1935 Reopened 1967

18 holes 6,025 yards S.S.S. 69

Green fees Apply to the Manager

Professional H. A. Padgham

Visiting societies Apply to Manager of Hotel

Meals All available, any time

Nearest railway station East Grinstead

R.A.C. (203)

Wilmerhatch Lane, Woodcote Park, Epsom, Surrey

Tel: Ashtead 76311

36 holes No. 1: 6,640 yards S.S.S. 72
No. 2: 5,548 yards S.S.S. 66
Both interesting parkland courses

Green fees From £1.75
Visitors with member welcome throughout week

Visiting societies Catered for midweek. Terms by arrangement

Meals Full catering and accommodation available by arrangement

Nearest railway station Epsom

ROYAL BLACKHEATH (204)

Court Road, Eltham, London SE9

Tel: 01-850 1795/1042

Founded 1608 Oldest golf club in the world 700 members

18 holes 6,024 yards S.S.S. 69 Slightly undulating parkland

Green fees Mon.-Fri. £2 per rd. £2.50 per day
Weekends £2.50 per rd. £3 per day
Public hols. £2.50 per rd. £3 per day
Introduction necessary

Professional George Johnson

Membership Full subscription £62.70 p.a. (E.F. £100)

Visiting societies Tues., Wed. and Thurs. only. £5.20

Meals Lunch and tea daily (except Mon.)

Nearest railway station Mottingham ¾ mile

Hotels in vicinity Bromley Court, Bromley

ROYAL CINQUE PORTS (205)

Golf Road, Deal, Kent

Tel: Deal 4007

Founded 1892 Venue for the British Open Championship, 1909 and 1920. Staged Amateur Championship 1923, English Amateur 1936 and 1950

18 holes 6,384 yards (medal tees)
6,659 yards (champs. tees) S.S.S. 72 Typical coastal, hummocky links course

Green fees Mon.-Fri. £2 per rd. £3 per day
Weekends £3.50 per rd. £4.50 per day

Professional Ian Morrison

Visiting societies Max. 60 Weekdays £5 per head
Weekends £6.85 per head

Meals Lunch and bar snacks daily

Nearest railway station Deal 2 miles

Hotels in vicinity Queen's, Royal and Clarendon, Deal; County, Canterbury

ROYAL EASTBOURNE (206)

Paradise Drive, Eastbourne, Sussex

Tel: Eastbourne 30412

Founded 1887 900 members

27 holes 6,063 yards S.S.S. 69 Undulating downland Also small 9-hole course

Green fees Mon.-Fri. £1.50
Weekends £2 (plus VAT)
Public hols. £2 (plus VAT)

Professional Neil Large

Membership Full subscription £35 p.a. (plus VAT) (E.F. £17.50)

Visiting societies By arrangement

Meals Lunch and tea (except Mon.)

Nearest railway station Eastbourne 1 mile

Hotels in vicinity Grand, Cavendish, Burlington and Cumberland, Eastbourne

ROYAL EPPING FOREST (207)

Forest Approach, Chingford, Essex

Tel: 01-529 2758

Founded 1888 400 members One of London's earliest clubs; royal prefix granted in 1889

18 holes 6,131 yards S.S.S. 69

Green fees Public course administered by Corporation of London

Professional R. Gowers

Visiting societies No facilities

Meals Bar snacks only

Nearest railway station Chingford 100 yards

Hotels in vicinity Royal Forest, Chingford; Roebuck, Buckhurst Hill

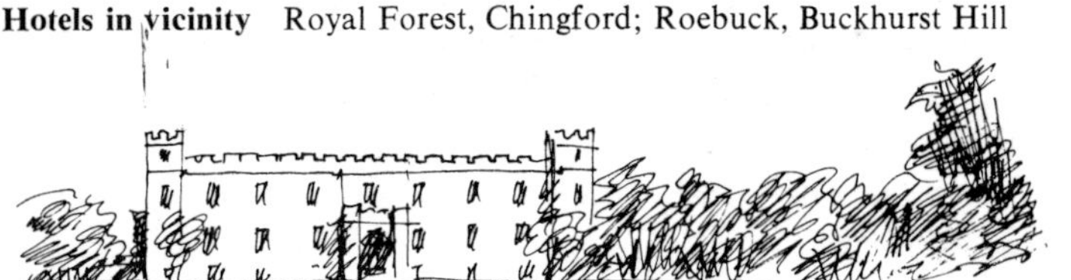

Syon House

ROYAL MID-SURREY (208)

Old Deer Park, Richmond, Surrey

Tel: 01-940 1894

36 holes Outer: 6,322 yards S.S.S. 70
Inner: 5,446 yards S.S.S. 70
Both fine parkland courses

Green fees Mon.-Fri. £2.75 per rd./day
Weekends no visitors
Introduction required

Professional D. Talbot

Visiting societies Terms by arrangement

Meals Lunch every day (except Mon.)

Nearest railway station Richmond (main line and District line tube) 400 yards

Hotels in vicinity Richmond Gate

ROYAL ST GEORGE'S (209)

Sandwich Bay, Kent

Tel: Sandwich 3090

18 holes 6,748 yards S.S.S. 72 Seaside

Green fees Mon.-Fri. £2.75 per rd.
Weekends £5.25 per rd./day
Visitors welcome on weekdays with member, not normally at weekends

Professional C. Whiting

Visiting societies Midweek only Terms on application

Meals Lunch daily (except Tues.)

Nearest railway station Sandwich

Hotels in vicinity Bell, Sandwich

ROYAL WIMBLEDON (210)

29 Camp Road, Wimbledon Common, London SW19

Tel: 01-946 0055

18 holes 6,300 yards S.S.S. 70 Parkland

Green fees Mon.-Fri. £2.75 per rd./day
Weekends with member only
Bona fide club members welcomed, if introduced

Professional R. Dailey

Visiting societies Wed. and Fri. only By arrangement

Meals Lunch daily (except Mon.)
Nearest railway station Wimbledon (main line and District line tube)

ROYAL WINCHESTER (211)

Sarum Road, Winchester, Hants.
Tel: Winchester 2462

Founded 1888 600 members The famous J. H. Taylor was club professional when he won British Open in 1894 and 1895

18 holes 6,039 yards S.S.S. 69 Chalk downland

Green fees Mon.-Fri. 75p per rd.
Weekends with member only
Introduction necessary

Professional A. E. Dedman

Visiting societies Limited to two societies per week. Apply to the Secretary

Meals Lunch, tea and dinner (except Thurs.)
Weekends, guests with members only

Nearest railway station Winchester 1 mile

Hotels in vicinity Southgate and Wessex, Winchester

ROYAL WORLINGTON & NEWMARKET (212)

Worlington, Bury St Edmunds, Suffolk
Tel: Mildenhall 712216

This is perhaps one of the most famous of 9-hole courses. It has been rated as the best in the world

9 holes 6,218 yards S.S.S. 70 Parkland

Green fees Mon.-Fri. £1.50 per rd. £2.25 per day
Weekends £3.75 per rd.
Bona fide club members only

Professional E. Beverley

Visiting societies Not catered for

Meals Lunch daily (except Mon.)

Nearest railway station Newmarket

Hotels in vicinity Bull, Barton Mills; Bell, Mildenhall

ROYSTON (213)

Baldock Road, Royston, Herts.
Tel: Royston 42177

Founded 1893 670 members

18 holes 5,984 yards S.S.S. 68 Undulating heathland

Green fees Mon.-Fri. £2
Weekends £2.50

Professional D. Astill (tel: Royston 43476)

Membership Full subscription £25 p.a. (E.F. £25)

Meals Full catering (except Wed.)
All meals by prior arrangement with the Stewardess

Nearest railway station Royston 1 mile

Hotels in vicinity Old Bull Inn and Banyers, Royston

RUISLIP (214)

Ickenham Road, Ruislip, Middx.

Tel: Ruislip 32004

Founded 1939

18 holes 5,187 yards S.S.S. 64 Flat wooded parkland
Municipal course with private club attached

Green fees Mon.-Fri. 75p
Weekends £1

Professional R. Walton

Membership Nominal subscription plus season ticket for municipal course

Visiting societies Not catered for

Meals Lunch available all week

Nearest railway station West Ruislip (Central line tube) 300 yards

Hotels in vicinity Master Brewer Motel, Hillingdon

RUSHDEN (215)

Chelveston, Northants.

Tel: Rushden 2581

9 holes 5,948 yards S.S.S. 68 Parkland

Green fees On application to the Secretary
Visitors welcome except Sun. a.m. and Sat. p.m.

Professional J. Wilson

Visiting societies Terms by arrangement

Meals Lunch (to be ordered 24 hours in advance)

Nearest railway station Chelveston

Hotels in vicinity Green Dragon, Higham Ferrars

RYE (216)

Camber, Rye, Sussex

Tel: Camber 241

18 holes 6,483 yards S.S.S. 72 Seaside

Green fees Visitors with member only
Mon.-Fri. £1.50 per day
Weekends £2 per day

Professional P. Marsh

Visiting societies Not catered for

Meals Lunch every day

Nearest railway station Rye

Hotels in vicinity Mermaid and Hope Anchor, Rye

SAFFRON WALDEN (217)

Windmill Hill, Saffron Walden, Essex

Tel: Saffron Walden 2116

9 holes 6,184 yards S.S.S. 69 Parkland

Green fees Mon.-Fri. £1.75 per day
Weekends £2.40 per day (with member only)

Professional G. Rand
Visiting societies Weekdays only. Terms by arrangement
Nearest railway station Audley End
Hotels in vicinity Cross Keys, Saffron Walden

Thaxted : The Guildhall

ST AUGUSTINE'S (218)

Cottington Road, Cliffsend, Ramsgate, Kent
Tel: Minster (Thanet) 346

Founded 1907 500 members
18 holes 5,226 yards S.S.S. 66 Links/parkland
Green fees Mon.-Fri. £1.65 per rd. £2.20 per day
Weekends £3.30 per rd./day
Professional S. H. Sherman
Membership Full subscription £27 p.a. (E.F. £50)
Visiting societies Max. 40 Terms by arrangement
Meals Full menu available any time
Nearest railway station Ramsgate 3 miles
Hotels in vicinity Eastways, Ramsgate

ST GEORGE'S HILL (219)

Weybridge, Surrey
Tel: Weybridge 42406

Founded 1912 500 members
27 holes Old (18): 6,507 yards S.S.S. 71
New (9): 2,706 yards S.S.S. 34
Pine and heather courses

Green fees Mon.-Fri. £2.75 (old) £1.10 (new)
Weekends £3.30 (old) £1.50 (new)
Letter of introduction necessary to play on Old Course

Professional A. C. Rattue

Membership Full subscription £88 p.a. (E.F. £88)

Visiting societies Wed. and Thurs. only. Terms by arrangement

Meals Lunch and tea every day (except Mon.)

Nearest railway station Weybridge ¾ mile

Hotels in vicinity Woodcourt, Cobham

SANDY LODGE (220)

Northwood, Middx.

Tel: Northwood 25429

Founded 1910 500 members

18 holes 6,430 yards S.S.S. 71 Sandy sub-soil

Green fees Mon.-Fri. £2.50 per rd. £4 per day
Weekends no visitors
Introduction necessary

Professional A. M. Fox

Visiting societies Max. 40 Weekdays only. £5.50 per head

Meals Lunch and tea every day (except Mon.)

Nearest railway station Moor Park (Metropolitan line tube) 200 yards

Hotels in vicinity Victoria, Rickmansworth; Caledonian, Watford

SELSEY (221)

Golf Links Lane, Selsey, Sussex

Tel: Selsey 2203

9 holes 5,654 yards S.S.S. 67 Seaside

Green fees Mon.-Fri. £1.25 per day
Weekends £2.20 per day
Visitors welcome except Sun. a.m.

Professional P. Sanders

Visiting societies Terms by arrangement

Meals Lunch daily

Nearest railway station Chichester

SEAFORD (222)

Firle Road, East Blatchington, Seaford, Sussex

Tel: Seaford 892442

18 holes 6,305 yards S.S.S. 70 Downland

Green fees Mon.-Fri. £2.20
Weekends £3.30
Visitors welcome all week except Sun. a.m.

Professional P. Brown

Visiting societies Weekdays only

Meals Lunch daily

Nearest railway station Seaford

Hotels in vicinity Dormy House and Esplanade, Seaford

SEAFORD HEAD (223)

Southdown Road, Seaford, Sussex

Tel: Seaford 890139

18 holes 5,812 yards S.S.S. 68 Seaside

Green fees Mon.-Fri. £1 per day
Weekends £1.40 per day
Bona fide club members welcome

Professional A. Lowles

Visiting societies Catered for by written appointment

Meals Lunch (by prior order)

Nearest railway station Seaford

Hotels in vicinity Seaford Head, Eversley, Mercury Motel, Viking Motel

SELSDON PARK (Hotel) (224)

Addington Road, South Croydon, Surrey CR2 8RA

Tel: 01-657 3127

18 holes 6,405 yards S.S.S. 72 Undulating parkland

Green fees Mon.-Fri. £2
Weekends from hotel only

Professional Bill Mitchell

Visiting societies Catered for weekdays and weekends after 12.30 p.m.

Meals Lunch in club Wed. and Thurs. Full catering in hotel

Nearest railway station Purley

Hotels in vicinity Selsdon Park

SENE VALLEY (Folkestone & Hythe) (225)

Sene, Folkestone, Kent

Tel: Hythe 66726

Founded 1888 Folkestone G.C. became Folkestone and Hythe G.C. in 1966

18 holes 6,754 yards S.S.S. 72 Downland course overlooking the sea. Designed by Henry Cotton and opened in 1966

Green fees Mon.-Fri. £2 per rd./day (£1 with member)
Weekends £3 per rd./day (£1.50 with member)
Introduction desirable but not essential

Professional C. Whiting

Membership Waiting list in operation for full membership. Other categories available; apply to the Secretary for details

Visiting societies Max. 50 Weekdays only. Terms by arrangement

Meals Full catering (except Mon.)

Nearest railway station Sandling Junction or Folkestone

Hotels in vicinity Imperial and Stade Court, Hythe

SHEERNESS (226)

Power Station Road, Sheerness, Kent ME12 3AE

Tel: Sheerness 2585

Founded 1902 by Royal Navy at H.M. Dockyard. Handed over to Town Council in 1908
350 members

18 holes 6,425 yards (formerly 9 holes, new layout to be completed by spring 1976)

Green fees Mon.-Fri. £1.10 per rd.
Weekends with member only
Bona fide club members only

Professional J. K. Young

Membership Full subscription £30 (E.F. £25)

Visiting societies Terms by arrangement

Meals By prior arrangement with the Steward

Nearest railway station Sheerness 1½ miles

Hotels in vicinity Royal Fountain and Blue Town, Sheerness

SHIRLEY PARK (227)

Addiscombe Road, Shirley Park, Croydon, Surrey CR0 7LB
Tel: 01-654 1143

Founded 1914 800 members

18 holes 6,283 yards S.S.S. 70 Parkland

Green fees Mon.-Fri. £1.65 per rd. £2.20 per day
Weekends with member only

Professional S. Parker

Membership Full subscription £50 p.a. (E.F. £60 plus VAT)

Visiting societies Max. 52 full day £4.50 per head inc.
Max. 36 half day £2.75 per head inc.

Meals Breakfast, lunch and tea daily (8 a.m.-6 p.m.)

Nearest railway station East Croydon 1 mile

SHOOTER'S HILL (228)

Lowood, Eaglesfield Road, London SE18 3DA
Tel: 01-854 1216

Founded 1903

18 holes 5,645 yards S.S.S. 67 Undulating, quite hilly

Green fees Mon.-Fri. £2 per day £1 per rd. (with member)
Weekends £1.50 (with member only)
Visitors must be introduced by and play with a member, or member of other club

Professional David Gray

Membership Closed

Visiting societies Max. 40 By arrangement. Green fee £2.50 per day (plus VAT) plus catering

Meals Available if booked in advance

Nearest railway station Blackheath 4 miles

Royal Naval College, Greenwich.

SHORTLANDS (229)

Shortlands, Bromley, Kent BR2 0PB

Tel: 01-460 2471

Founded 1897 Originally opened as ladies' golf club

9 holes 5,216 yards S.S.S. 65 Flat parkland

Green fees Mon.-Fri. £1 per day (reduction with member)
Weekends no visitors
Bona fide club members only

Professional J. Spivey

Membership Full subscription £153 p.a. (E.F. £50); Ladies £50 p.a. (E.F. £40)

Visiting societies Not catered for

Meals Daily (except Mon.)

Nearest railway station Shortlands 500 yards

Hotels in vicinity Crest, Hackwood and Bromley Court, Bromley

SIDCUP (230)

Hurst Road, Sidcup, Kent DA15 9AE

Tel: 01-300 2150

9 holes 5,632 yards S.S.S. 68 Fairly flat course with River Shuttle and lake affecting 5 holes

Green fees Mon.-Fri. £1.15 per rd.
Weekends no visitors

Professional J. Lane

Visiting societies Not catered for

Meals Bar snacks every day (except Wed.)

Nearest railway station Sidcup under ½ mile

Hotels in vicinity Railway, Sidcup

SITTINGBOURNE & MILTON REGIS (231)

Wormdale, Newington, Sittingbourne, Kent ME9 7PX

Tel: Newington 842261

Founded 1929 600 members

18 holes 6,242 yards S.S.S. 70 Rolling downland overlooking orchards, farms and River Swale

Green fees Mon.-Fri. £1.50 per rd./day
Sat. £2 per rd./day
Sun. with member only

Professional J. R. Hearn

Membership Full subscription £34 p.a. (E.F. £34)
Applicants must have handicap

Visiting societies Max. 50 Green fees £2 per day
Catering by arrangement

Meals All meals available

Nearest railway station Newington $1\frac{1}{2}$ miles

Hotels in vicinity Coniston, Sittingbourne

SONNING (232)

Duffield Road, Sonning, Berks.

Tel: Reading 693332

Founded 1914 700 members

18 holes 6,349 yards S.S.S. 70 Parkland

Green fees Mon.-Fri. £2.20 per day (£1.65 with member)
Weekends with member only
Introduction necessary

Professional H. A. J. Young

Membership Full subscription £35 p.a. (E.F. nil)

Visiting societies Limited number, £5 per head

Meals Available on prior application

Nearest railway station Reading or Twyford

Hotels in vicinity White Hart and French Horn, Sonning

SOUTH BEDFORDSHIRE (233)

Warden Hill, Barton Road, Luton, Beds. LU2 7AA

Tel: Luton 55201

Founded 1884 500 members

18 holes 6,225 yards S.S.S. 70

Green fees Mon.-Fri. £1.65 per day
Weekends £2.50 (when available) contact Secretary

Professional L. A. Titterington

Membership Full subscription £28 p.a. (E.F. £40)

Visiting societies 20-50 persons, by arrangement

Meals Available at all times

Nearest railway station Luton 2 miles

Hotels in vicinity Esso, Strathmore and others in town centre

Comments Midweek Medals—some Wed.
Ladies' Day—Tues.

SOUTH HERTS. (234)

Links Drive, Totteridge, London N20

Tel: 01-445 7325

Founded 1899 Harry Vardon was first club professional

18 holes 6,449 yards S.S.S. 71 Undulating parkland

Green fees Mon.-Fri. on application to the Secretary
Weekends with member only

Professional Dai Rees O.B.E.

Membership Waiting list

Visiting societies Terms on application

Meals Lunch daily

Nearest railway station Totteridge & Whetstone (Northern line tube)

Hotels in vicinity West Lodge Park, Hadley Wood

SOUTHFIELD (235)

Hill Top Road, Headington, Oxford

Tel: Oxford 42158

Founded 1875 Home of the Oxford University G.C., Oxford G.C. and Oxford Ladies G.C.

18 holes 6,210 yards S.S.S. 70 Undulating parkland

Green fees Mon.-Fri. £2.20 (with member £1.65)
Weekends £2.75 with member only

Professional Tony Rees

Membership Waiting list

Visiting societies Approx. £3.75 per head according to requirements

Meals Full catering (except Mon. and Tues.)

Nearest railway station Oxford 3 miles

Hotels in vicinity Eastgate, Oxford

SOUTHSEA (236)

Great Salterns, Eastern Road, Portsmouth, Hants.

Tel: Portsmouth 64549

Founded 1914 (re-founded 1972) Plays over municipal course, Great Salterns. Administered by Portsmouth Dept. of Leisure Services. Southsea G.C. organises competitive golf on the course
300 members

18 holes 6,018 yards S.S.S. 69 Flat seaside

Green fees Mon.-Fri. 65p per rd.
Weekends 85p per rd.

Professional W. McHardy

Membership Full subscription £2 p.a. (E.F. £1)
Plus season ticket for municipal course

Visiting societies Charges as per green fees

Meals Not available

Nearest railway station Fratton 1 mile

Hotels in vicinity Numerous hotels in Southsea

STANMORE (237)

Gordon Avenue, Stanmore, Middx.

Tel: 01-954 2599

Founded 1893 560 members

18 holes 5,925 yards S.S.S. 68 Hilly parkland

Green fees Tues.-Thurs. £2.20 per rd. £3.30 per day
Weekends with member only £1 per rd. £1.65 per day

Professional V. R. Law

Membership Full subscription £48 p.a. (E.F. £48)

Visiting societies Max. 40 Weekdays only. £5.50 approx. per head

Meals Full catering every day (except Mon.)

Nearest railway station Harrow & Wealdstone or Stanmore
(Bakerloo line tube)

STOKE BY NAYLAND (238)

Keepers Lane, Leaven Heath, Colchester, Essex

Tel: Nayland 262836

Founded 1973 600 members

18 holes 6,523 yards S.S.S. 71 Open rolling parkland with abundance of water
Planning permission has been granted for further 18 holes

Green fees Mon.-Fri. £1.65 per day
Weekends apply to Secretary in advance
Bona fide club members only

Professional Chester Jarvis

Membership Full subscription £50 p.a. (E.F. £40)

Visiting societies Max. 60 Welcome during week. Approx. £4.50 per head

Meals Lunch, dinner and bar snacks every day

Nearest railway station Colchester 10 miles

Hotels in vicinity Talbooth, Dedham; Old Mill, Sudbury

STOKE POGES (239)

Stoke Poges, Slough, Bucks.

Tel: Slough 26385

Founded 1909 700 members

18 holes 6,646 yards S.S.S. 72 Wooded parkland

Green fees Mon.Fri. £3.25 per day (£2 after 4 p.m.)
Weekends no visitors

Professional Jim Lynch

Membership Full subscription £77 p.a. (E.F. £77)

Visiting societies Max. 72 £6.60 per head

Meals Lunch daily except Mon., to be ordered by 11 a.m.
Mon.—snacks only

Nearest railway station Slough

Hotels in vicinity Bell House, Beaconsfield; Bull, Gerrard's Cross

STRAWBERRY HILL (240)

Wellesley Road, Strawberry Hill, Twickenham, Middx.

Tel: 01-894 1246

9 holes 4,690 yards S.S.S. 63 Parkland

Green fees Mon.-Fri. £1.15
Weekends no visitors

Professional T. Bowden

Visiting societies Not catered for

Meals Lunch daily

Nearest railway station Strawberry Hill

SUDBURY (241)

Bridgewater Road, Wembley, Middx.

Tel: 01-902 0218

Founded 1920 480 members

18 holes 6,282 yards S.S.S. 70 Wooded parkland

Green fees Mon.-Fri. £3 per rd./day
Weekends with member only

Professional Tony Fisher

Membership Full subscription £65 p.a. (E.F. £75)

Visiting societies Tues. and Thurs. only. Terms by arrangement

Meals Lunch and tea every day (except Mon.)

Nearest railway station Sudbury Town (Piccadilly line tube) ½ mile

Hotels in vicinity Esso Motor, Wembley

SUNDRIDGE PARK (242)

Garden Road, Bromley, Kent

Tel: 01-460 0278

Founded 1901 The courses were opened by the then Prime
Minister, Mr Balfour. 1,250 members

36 holes East: 6,310 yards S.S.S. 70 } well-wooded
West: 6,027 yards S.S.S. 69 } parkland

Green fees Mon.-Fri. £3.10 per rd. £4.60 per day
Weekends no visitors
Introduction necessary

Professional George Will

Membership Full subscription £70 p.a. (E.F. £100)
Further details on application

Visiting societies Max. 48 Tues. and Thurs. only. £6.82 per head, fully inc.

Meals Full day menu always available, evening meals by arrangement

Nearest railway station Sundridge Park 300 yards

Hotels in vicinity Bromley Court, Bromley Continental and Grianan, Bromley

SUNNINGDALE (243)

Ascot, Berks.

Tel: Ascot 21681

Founded 1901 Famous venue for top professional tournaments. Also Sunningdale Foursomes, Golf Illustrated Gold Vase, Dunlop Masters, English Ladies' Championship, Colgate European Women's Open
770 members

36 holes Old: 6,336 yards S.S.S. 70 } heather and pine
New: 6,601 yards S.S.S. 72 } on heathland

Green fees Mon.-Fri. £1.75 per day (with member)
1 Nov.-31 Mar £4 per day
1 April-31 Oct. £4.50 per day
Weekends £2.25 with member only
Visitors with written introduction

Professional Arthur Lees

Membership Full subscription £80 p.a. (E.F. £220)

Visiting societies Max. 100 £7 per head

Meals Lunch and tea (except Mon.)
(Lunch £1.50, tea 30p)

Nearest railway station Sunningdale (easy walking distance)

Hotels in vicinity Cricketers', Bagshot; Berystede and Royal Berkshire, Ascot

SUNNINGDALE LADIES (244)

Cross Road, Sunningdale, Berks.

Tel: Ascot 20507

18 holes 3,624 yards S.S.S. 60 Heathland, specially designed for ladies' golf

Green fees Mon.-Fri. £1 (reduction if introduced by member)

Visiting societies Ladies' societies catered for. Terms by arrangement

Meals Light lunch available every day, to be ordered by 11 a.m.

Nearest railway station Sunningdale

SURBITON (245)

Woodstock Lane, Chessington, Surrey

Tel: 01-398 3101

18 holes 6,211 yards S.S.S. 70 Parkland

Green fees Mon.-Fri. £2.75 per day
Visitors welcome
Weekends introduced by and playing with member

Professional J. A. Meadon

Visiting societies Terms by arrangement

Meals Lunch daily

Nearest railway station Chessington

Hotels in vicinity Bear and Moore

TADMARTON HEATH (246)

Wigginton, Banbury, Oxon.

Tel: Hook Norton 278

18 holes 5,886 yards S.S.S. 68 Heathland

Green fees Mon.-Fri. £1.65
Weekends £1.15 with member only

Professional D. King

Visiting societies Terms by arrangement

Meals Lunch daily (except Mon.)

Nearest railway station Banbury

Hotels in vicinity Whateley Hall and White Lion, Banbury; Wroxton Hotel, Wroxton

TANDRIDGE (247)

Oxted, Surrey

Tel: Oxted 2273

Founded 1924 650 members

18 holes 6,429 yards S.S.S. 70 Parkland

Green fees Mon.-Thurs. £1.90 per rd. £3 per day
Fri.-Sun. with members only
Introduction necessary

Professional A. J. Baker

Membership By invitation of member only

Visiting societies Max. 40 £5.50 per day (booking 1-2 years in advance)

Meals Lunch and tea every day

Nearest railway station Oxted 1 mile

Hotels in vicinity Hoskins Arms, Oxted

TEMPLE (248)

Henley Road, Hurley, Nr Maidenhead, Berks.

Tel: Littlewick Green 4248

Founded 1904

18 holes 6,133 yards S.S.S. 69 Parkland

Green fees Mon.-Fri. £3.30
Weekends no visitors
Introduction required

Professional G. W. Cox

Membership Waiting list up to 2 years

Visiting societies Max. 40 £6 per head, inc.

Meals Lunch Tues.-Fri. (prior booking required), snacks all week

Nearest railway station Maidenhead 3 miles

Hotels in vicinity Compleat Angler, Marlow; Old Belle, Hurley

Comments The former Open Champion, Henry Cotton, was professional here until 1971

TENTERDEN (249)

Woodchurch Road, Tenterden, Kent

Tel: Tenterden 2660

Founded 1905 340 members

9 holes 5,119 yards S.S.S. 65 Scenic with good views of North Downs

Green fees Mon.-Fri. £1.10 per rd.
Weekends £1.65
No visitors before 12 noon on Sun.

Membership Full subscription £16.50 (E.F. £11.50)

Visiting societies By arrangement

Meals Not catered for

Nearest railway station Headcorn 8 miles

Hotels in vicinity White Lion, Tenterden

THAMES DITTON & ESHER (250)

Marquis of Granby Hotel, Portsmouth Road, Esher, Surrey

Tel: 01-398 1551

Founded 1892 220 members

9 holes 5,300 yards S.S.S. 66 Common land

Green fees Mon.-Fri. 75p (18 holes)
Weekends £1.25 (18 holes)

Professional R. Hutton (tournament)

Membership Full subscription £16.50 p.a. (E.F. £22)

Visiting societies By arrangement

Meals No catering available

Nearest railway station Esher 500 yards

Hotels in vicinity Marquis of Granby

THEYDON BOIS (251)

Theydon Road, Epping, Essex CM16 4EH

Tel: Theydon Bois 3054

Founded 1897 600 members

18 holes 5,030 metres S.S.S. 67
9 holes Epping Forest land, 9 holes new parkland

Green fees Mon.-Fri. £1.45
Weekends £2.75 (not Sun. a.m.)
Only bona fide club members

Professional D. Edgar

Membership Full subscription £55 p.a. (E.F. £55) inc. VAT

Visiting societies Max. 40 £4.70 per head inc. green fees, lunch and dinner

Meals All available every day

Nearest railway station Theydon Bois 1 mile

Hotels in vicinity Bell Motel and Epping Forest Motel, Epping

THORNDON PARK (252)

Thorndon Park, Ingrave, Brentwood, Essex CM13 3RH
Tel: Horndon Green 666

18 holes 6,392 yards S.S.S. 71 Parkland

Green fees Mon.-Fri. £2.25 per rd. £3.25 per day
prior permission necessary
Weekends with member only

Professional R. Plumbridge

Visiting societies Rarely catered for Terms by arrangement

Meals Lunch every day (except Mon.)

Nearest railway station Brentwood

Hotels in vicinity Lion & Lamb, Brentwood

THORPE HALL (253)

Thorpe Hall Avenue, Thorpe Bay, Essex
Tel: Southend-on-Sea 582205

Founded 1907 1,065 members

18 holes 6,247 yards (5,712 metres) S.S.S. 71
Parkland

Green fees Mon.-Fri. £2.50 per rd. £3 per day
Weekends with member only
Bona fide club members only; handicap cert. essential

Professional Roger Smith

Membership Full subscription £63 p.a. (E.F. £60)

Visiting societies On application to the Secretary

Meals Full catering facilities

Nearest railway station Thorpe Bay ½ mile

Hotels in vicinity Airport, Southend-on-Sea; Roslin, Thorpe Bay

THREE RIVERS (254)

Stow Road, Cold Norton, Nr Purleigh, Essex
Tel: Purleigh 631

Founded 1973 500 members Country club

18 holes 6,625 yards S.S.S. 72 Parkland
9 hole par 3

Green fees Mon.-Fri. £2.20 per rd. £3.30 per day
with member, £1.10 per rd. £1.65 per day
Weekends £1.65 and £2.20 with member only

Professional G. Christie

Membership Full subscription £90 p.a. (E.F. £120)

Visiting societies No limit on numbers
Charges as per green fees plus meals by arrangement

Meals Restaurant, Grill Room, private dining facilities. Available all week

Nearest railway station Woodham Ferrers 3 miles

Hotels in vicinity Marks Tey, Colchester

TYRRELLS WOOD (255)

Tyrrells Wood, Leatherhead, Surrey

Tel: Leatherhead 73687

18 holes 6,230 yards S.S.S. 70

Green fees Mon.-Fri. £2 per rd./day
Sat. £3 per rd./day (£1.50 with member)
Sun. £4 per rd./day
Letter of introduction necessary unless bona fide club member

Professional E. W. Ward

Visiting societies Tues.-Fri. only. Terms by arrangement

Meals Lunch every day (except Mon.)

Nearest railway station Leatherhead

Hotels in vicinity Burford Bridge, Dorking; Bull, Leatherhead

UPMINSTER (256)

Hall Lane, Upminster, Essex

Tel: Upminster 22788

Founded 1928 650 members Clubhouse over 900 years old

18 holes 5,951 yards S.S.S. 69 Parkland

Green fees Mon.-Fri. only £2.50 per rd. £3.50 per day
Bona fide club members only; handicap cert. essential

Professional N. Carr

Membership Waiting list

Visiting societies Max. 45 £2.60 Charges as per green fee plus catering requirements

Meals Full restaurant facilities

Nearest railway station Upminster (District line tube) ½ mile

Hotels in vicinity Fairlane Motel, Upminster

UXBRIDGE (257)

The Drive, Harefield Place, Uxbridge, Middx.

Tel: Uxbridge 33160

18 holes 5,500 yards S.S.S. 67 Parkland

Green fees Mon.-Fri. 60p
Weekends 85p
Visitors welcome without reservation

Visiting societies Catered for at all times

Meals Light meals available

Nearest railway station Uxbridge (Piccadilly and Metropolitan line tube) 2 miles

Hotels in vicinity Denham Lodge and Master Brewer Motel, Hillingdon

VERULAM (258)

London Road, St Albans, Herts.

Tel: St Alban's 53327

Founded 1905 Home club of Samuel Ryder, Captain in 1911
570 members

18 holes 6,270 yards S.S.S. 70 Parkland

Green fees Mon.-Fri. £2 per rd. £2.50 per day
Weekends introduced by and playing with member only

Professional D. Snowdon

Visiting societies Terms by arrangement

Meals Full catering (except Mon.)

Nearest railway station St Albans City ¾ mile

Hotels in vicinity Sopwell House, Great Red Lion, Peahen and White Hart, St Albans

WALMER & KINGSDOWN (259)

The Leas, Kingsdown, Deal, Kent

Tel: Deal 3256

Founded 1909 Course designed by James Braid

18 holes 6,488 yards S.S.S. 71 Set on chalk cliffs, with magnificent views across Goodwin Sands

Green fees Mon.-Fri. £1.50 per day
Weekends £2.50 per day
Bona fide club members welcomed

Professional M. P. Lee

Membership Full subscription £45 p.a. (E.F. £20)

Visiting societies Max. 30 Weekdays only. Terms by arrangement

Meals Lunch and tea daily

Nearest railway station Walmer 3 miles

Hotels in vicinity Glen, Walmer; Blencathra, Kingsdown

WALTON HEATH (260)

Tadworth, Surrey

Tel: Tadworth 2060

Founded 1905 750 members James Braid was professional for 45 years. Venue for numerous top amateur events including British Ladies' Championships, English Match and Stroke Play Championships, and Golf Illustrated Gold Vase

36 holes Old: 6,837 yards S.S.S. 73 } Heather, pine and birch
New: 6,739 yards S.S.S. 72 } fast fairways

Green fees Mon.-Fri. £3.85 per day
Weekends with member only
Introduction necessary, please enquire in advance

Professional Harry Busson

Visiting societies Weekdays only. Charges on application. Early booking advisable due to demand

Meals Lunch and tea daily

Nearest railway station Tadworth 1 mile

Hotels in vicinity Drift Bridge, Epsom; Burford Bridge, Dorking; Copthorne; Tadworth Country Club

WANSTEAD (261)

Overton Drive, Wanstead, London E11 1NS

Tel: 01-989 3938

Founded 1893 400 members

18 holes 6,262 yards S.S.S. 70 Parkland

Green fees Mon.-Fri. £2 per rd. (plus VAT)
Weekends by invitation and with member only

Professional R. A. Knight

Membership Full subscription £42 p.a. (E.F. £25)

Visiting societies Max. 40 £6.50 per day, all inc.

Meals April to October, full catering

Nearest railway station Wanstead ½ mile

Hotels in vicinity Cromer Lodge

WARREN (262)

Woodham Walter, Maldon, Essex CM9 6RW

Tel: Danbury 3258/3198

Founded 1932 600 members

18 holes 6,285 yards S.S.S. 70 Picturesque course, area-wooded parkland

Green fees Mon.-Fri. £2 per rd. £3 per day
Weekends £3 (after midday only)
Introduction necessary

Professional J. R. Newman

Membership Full subscription £53.25 p.a. (E.F. £66)
All categories available on application

Visiting societies Max. 36 Charges as per green fees, meals by arrangement

Meals Full service all week

Nearest railway station Chelmsford 6 miles

Hotels in vicinity Blue Boar, Maldon; South Lodge and County, Chelmsford

WATERHALL (263)

Mill Road, Brighton, Sussex BN1 8YN

Tel: Brighton 508658

350 members Playing over public course

18 holes 5,213 yards S.S.S. 65 Downland

Green fees Mon.-Fri. £1 per rd. £1.30 per day
after 5 p.m. 65p per rd.
Weekends £1.30 per rd.
Public hols. £1.30 per rd.

Professional E. Charman

Visiting societies Mon.-Fri. only. Charges as per green fees, plus catering according to requirements (no catering Tues.)

Meals Bar snacks available
Cooked meals 24 hours' notice required. Golfers only

Nearest railway station Brighton, Hove, Portslade

Hotels in vicinity Numerous hotels in Brighton and Hove

WATERLOOVILLE (264)

Waterlooville, Hants.

Tel: Waterlooville 3388/52661

Founded 1907 700 members

18 holes 5,210 yards S.S.S. 65 Parkland

Green fees Mon.-Fri. £1.65 per rd. £2.20 per day
Weekends no visitors

Professional S. Barnes

Membership Full subscription £33 p.a. (E.F. £33)

Visiting societies Max. 60 £5 all inc. (p.m. £3.50 with tea)

Meals Lunch (24 hours' notice required for cooked meals)

Nearest railway station Cosham 5 miles

WELLINGBOROUGH (265)

Harrowdean Road, Wellingborough, Northants.

Tel: Wellingborough 2080

Founded 1892 340 members

9 holes 5,280 yards S.S.S. 68 Parkland

Green fees Mon.-Fri. £1 per rd (75p with member)
Weekends £1 with member only

Professional R. A. King

Membership Full subscription £24.20 p.a. (E.F. £27.50)
Lists closed

Visiting societies Not catered for

Meals Available, by prior arrangement with the Steward

Nearest railway station Wellingborough 2 miles

Hotels in vicinity Hind, Wellingborough

Comments A new 18-hole course is at present under construction at Harrowden Hall, 2 miles outside Wellingborough on the Kettering road. It is unlikely that visitors will be permitted on the new course until 1976.

WELWYN GARDEN CITY (266)

Mannicotts, High Oaks Road, Welwyn Garden City, Herts.

Tel: Welwyn Garden 25243

Founded 1923 650 members

18 holes 6,152 yards S.S.S. 69

Green fees Mon.-Fri. £1.50 per rd. £2.50 per day
Weekends no visitors

Professional I. Connelly

Membership Full subscription £40 p.a. (E.F. £40)

Visiting societies Max. 60 £4.50 per head inc.

Meals Lunch and high tea by prior arrangement

Nearest railway station Welwyn Garden City ½ mile

Hotels in vicinity Homestead Court and Treetops, Welwyn Garden City

WENTWORTH (267)

Virginia Water, Surrey

Tel: Wentworth 2201

36 holes East: 6,202 yards S.S.S. 70
West: 6,997 yards S.S.S. 73
The famous 'Burma Road' venue for numerous top professional and amateur events

9 holes 1,731 yards Par 30

Green fees Mon.-Fri. £3.30 per rd. (£1.40 with member) by prior application only
Weekends with member only

Professional T. Haliburton

Membership Lists closed

Visiting societies Advance booking essential

Meals Full catering all year round

Nearest railway station Virginia Water within 1 mile

Hotels in vicinity Berystede, Royal Foresters and Royal Berkshire, Ascot; Great Fosters and Runnymede, Egham

WEST BYFLEET (268)

Sheerwater Road, West Byfleet, Surrey

Tel: Byfleet 45230

Founded 1922 590 members

18 holes 6,320 yards S.S.S. 70 Woodland and gorse

Green fees Charges on application
Introduction preferred

Professional P. Cheal

Membership Lists closed

Visiting societies Terms by arrangement

Meals Lunch daily, prior notice required

Nearest railway station West Byfleet

Hotels in vicinity Crown's House (2 min. from club)

WEST ESSEX (269)

Bury Road, Sewardstonebury, Chingford, Essex

Tel: 01-529 7558

Founded 1900 560 members Venue for numerous county competitions

36 holes Blue: 5,897 yards S.S.S. 68
Yellow: 6,325 yards S.S.S. 70
Parkland course fringing on Epping Forest

Green fees Mon.-Fri. £2 per rd. (£1.50 with member)
£2.75 per day (£2 with member)
Weekends with member only

Professional M. N. R. Plumbridge

Visiting societies By arrangement; charges vary according to catering requirements

Meals Full catering (except Mon.)

Nearest railway station Chingford $1\frac{3}{4}$ miles

Hotels in vicinity Bell Motel, Epping

WEST HERTS. (270)

Rousebarn Lane, Cassiobury Park, Watford, Herts.

Tel: Watford 24264

18 holes 6,482 yards S.S.S. 72 Parkland

Green fees Mon.-Fri. fees on application
Weekends with member only

Professional R. Mandeville

Visiting societies Weekdays only Terms by arrangement

Meals Lunch daily (by prior arrangement with the Chief Steward)

Hotels in vicinity Two Brewers and Southern Cross, Watford

WEST HILL (271)

Brookwood, Surrey

Tel: Brookwood 2110

Founded 1909 450 members

18 holes 6,407 yards S.S.S. 71 Pine, silver birch and heather

Green fees Mon.-Fri. £3.30 per rd./day
Weekends £5.50 per rd./day
Introduction necessary

Professional C. G. Pennington

Visiting societies £6 per head, not on Mon. or Fri.

Meals Available all week
Nearest railway station Brookwood ¾ mile
Hotels in vicinity Worplesdon Place

WEST HOVE (272)

Old Shoreham Road, Hove, Brighton, Sussex
Tel: Brighton 419738 (Secretary)

Founded 1910 400 members
18 holes 6,040 yards S.S.S. 69 Downland
Green fees Mon.-Fri. £1.10 per rd./£1.65 per day
Weekends £2.20 per rd./£3.50 per day
Professional G. Shepherd (tel: Brighton 413494)
Membership Full subscription £10 p.a. (E.F. £35 plus VAT)
Visiting societies Max. 60 £4.50 per head all inc.
Meals Full restaurant
Nearest railway station West Hove
Hotels in vicinity Dudley, Hove

WEST KENT (273)

Downe, Nr Orpington, Kent
Tel: Downe 53737

450 members
18 holes 6,368 yards S.S.S. 70 Well-wooded
Green fees Mon.-Fri. £2 per day
Weekends no visitors
Introduction necessary
Professional R. S. Fidler
Membership Full subscription £65 p.a. (E.F. £90)
Visiting societies Max. 40 £6.50 per head
Meals Daily (except Mon. and Fri.)
Nearest railway station Orpington 4 miles
Hotels in vicinity George, Farnborough

WEST MIDDLESEX (274)

Greenford Road, Southall, Middx.
Tel: 01-574 3450

Founded 1894 500 members
18 holes 6,176 yards S.S.S. 69 Parkland

Green fees Mon.-Fri. £2 per rd./day
Weekends £3 per rd./day

Professional K. Wells

Membership Full subscription £44 p.a. (E.F. £25)

Visiting societies Weekdays only. £5 per head approx.

Meals Lunch every day (except Mon.)

Nearest railway station Hanwell 1½ miles

Hotels in vicinity All West London hotels within 20 minutes by car

WEST SURREY (275)

Enton Green, Godalming, Surrey
Tel: Godalming 21275

Founded 1910 500 members

18 holes 6,245 yards S.S.S. 70 Parkland

Green fees Mon.-Fri. £2.20 per rd./day
Weekends £3.30 per rd./day
Reductions if playing with member
Bona fide club members only

Professional P. Thubron

Membership Full subscription £54 p.a. (E.F. £54)

Visiting societies Limited Green fees plus catering requirements
Full terms on application

Meals Lunch and tea daily (except Mon.)

Nearest railway station Milford ¼ mile

Hotels in vicinity Crown, Chiddingfold; Lake, Godalming

Parham.

WEST SUSSEX (276)

Storrington Road, Pulborough, Sussex

Tel: Pulborough 2563

750 members

18 holes 6,214 yards S.S.S. 70 Wooded downland

Green fees Mon.-Fri. £2.50 per day
Weekends £2.50 per day
Introduction necessary

Professional G. Gledhill

Membership Lists full

Visiting societies £5 per head per day inc.
Limited nos. Please apply to Secretary

Meals Available

Nearest railway station Pulborough 3 miles

Hotels in vicinity Roundabout, West Chiltington

WESTGATE & BIRCHINGTON (277)

Westgate-on-Sea, Kent

Tel: Thanet 31115

18 holes 4,926 yards S.S.S. 65 Links

Green fees Mon.-Fri. £1.25 per day
Weekends £1.75 per day
Bona fide club members only
Reduction when playing with a member

Professional R. Game

Visiting societies By arrangement

Meals By prior arrangement only

Nearest railway station Westgate-on-Sea

Hotels in vicinity Bungalow, Birchington-on-Sea

WHITELEAF (278)

White Leaf, Princes Risborough, Bucks.

Tel: Princes Risborough 3097

Founded 1904 250 members

9 holes 5,359 yards S.S.S. 66 Hilly, surrounded by beech woods, short but testing

Green fees Mon.-Fri. £1.50 per rd. £2.20 per day
Weekends no visitors

Professional Ken Ward

Membership 170 male Sub. £30 plus VAT (E.F. £30)
80 ladies Sub. £21 plus VAT (E.F. £21)

Visiting societies None

Meals Every day (except Mon.)

Nearest railway station Princes Risborough 2 miles

Hotels in vicinity Shoulder of Mutton, Owlswick; George and Dragon, Princes Risborough; Bernard Arms, Great Kimble

WHITEWEBBS (279)

Beggars Hollow, Clay Hill, Enfield, Middx.

Tel: 01-363 3455

Founded 1932 325 members

18 holes 5,809 yards S.S.S. 68 Parkland

Green fees Mon.-Fri. 40p
Weekends 50p

Professional D. Lewis

Membership Private club playing over municipal course

Visiting societies Not catered for

Meals Available

Nearest railway station Gordon Hill

Hotels in vicinity Royal Chase, Enfield; West Lodge, Hadley Wood

WILDERNESSE (280)

Seal, Sevenoaks, Kent

Tel: Sevenoaks 61199

Founded 1890 850 members

18 holes 6,648 yards S.S.S. 71 Very scenic undulating woodland

Green fees Mon.-Fri. £3 per day £1.75 per rd. if introduced
Introduction required at all times

Professional W. Dawson

Visiting societies Restricted. Terms by arrangement

Meals Full menu daily

Nearest railway station Sevenoaks 2 miles

Hotels in vicinity Crossways and Moorings, Sevenoaks

WILLINGDON (281)

Southdown Road, Eastbourne

Tel: Eastbourne 32383

Founded 1898 520 members

18 holes 5,466 yards S.S.S. 69 Downland

Green fees Mon.-Fri. £1.50
Weekends £2
Public hols. £2

Professional Donald Ross

Membership Full subscription £35 (plus VAT) p.a. (E.F. £17.50)

Visiting societies Max. 40 £3.75 per head per day

Meals Lunch and tea every day (except Mon.)
Prior notice for lunch is appreciated

Nearest railway station Eastbourne 2 miles

WIMBLEDON COMMON (282)

Camp Road, Wimbledon Common, London SW19

Tel: 01-946 0294

18 holes 5,424 yards S.S.S. 66 Common land

Green fees Mon.-Fri. 85p (with member 55p)
Weekends £1.75 (with member 90p)
Bona fide club members welcomed

Visiting societies Not usually catered for

Meals Lunch available Tues. and Sat. (to be ordered before 10 a.m.)

Nearest railway station Wimbledon (main line and District line tube)

Hotels in vicinity Within easy access London, West End

WIMBLEDON PARK (283)

Home Park Road, Wimbledon, London SW19

Tel: 01-946 1250

Founded 1899

18 holes 5,450 yards S.S.S. 66 Parkland

Green fees Mon.-Fri. £3
Weekends introduced and playing with member only

Professional F. C. Lucas

Visiting societies Terms by arrangement

Meals Lunch available Tues.-Fri. only

Nearest railway station Wimbledon Park (District line tube) 5 mins.

WOKING (284)

Hook Heath, Woking, Surrey

Tel: Woking 60053

18 holes 6,300 yards S.S.S. 70 Parkland

Green fees Mon.-Fri. £1.50 per rd.
Weekends with member only
Introduction necessary
Bona fide club members only

Professional J. Thorne

Visiting societies Terms by arrangement

Meals Lunch and tea (prior booking essential)

Nearest railway station Woking

WOODCOTE PARK (285)

Bridle Way, Meadow Hill, Coulsdon, Surrey

Tel: 01-688 2788

Founded 1912

18 holes 6,592 yards S.S.S. 71 Plateau and woodland

Green fees Mon.-Fri. £2 per rd. (£2.50 per day)
Weekends with member only

Professional I. Martin

Membership Full subscription £50 p.a. (E.F. £75)

Visiting societies Green fees as above, plus meal charges by arrangement

Meals Lunch only (to be ordered by 10 a.m.)

Nearest railway station Purley 2 miles

Hotels in vicinity Red Lion, Coulsdon

WOODFORD (286)

Sunset Avenue, Woodford Green, Essex

Tel: 01-504 0553

Founded 1890 380 members

9 holes 5,689 yards S.S.S. 67

Green fees Mon.-Fri. £1.50 per rd./day 18 holes
no green fees Tues. or Thurs. a.m.
Weekends with member only

Professional L. Burgess

Membership Full subscription £35 p.a. (E.F. £25)

Visiting societies Not catered for

Meals Bar snacks available

Nearest railway station Woodford

WORPLESDON (287)

Heath House Lane, Woking, Surrey

Tel: Brookwood 2277

Founded 1908 500 members

18 holes 6,422 yards S.S.S. 71 Heather and parkland

Green fees Mon.-Fri. £3.30 per rd.
Weekends £5.50 per rd.
At discretion of the Secretary

Professional A. Waters

Visiting societies £6 per head (men)
£5 per head (ladies)
Numbers by arrangement

Meals Lunch and bar snacks

Nearest railway station Brookwood 1 mile

Hotels in vicinity Mayford Manor, Worplesdon Place and Cotteridge, Woking

WORTHING (288)

Links Road, Worthing, Sussex

Tel: Worthing 60801

Founded 1905 1,000 members

36 holes Upper: 5,127 yards S.S.S. 65
Lower: 6,274 yards S.S.S. 70

Green fees Mon.-Fri. £3.30 (with member £1.10)
Weekends £5.50 (with member £1.65)
Public hols. £5.50 (with member £1.65)

Professional E. G. Boone

Membership Full subscription £40 p.a. (E.F. £60)

Visiting societies On application

Meals Full restaurant, but advance booking necessary

Nearest railway station Worthing Central 1½ miles approx.

Hotels in vicinity Eardley, Chatsworth, Warnes and many others in central Worthing

WROTHAM HEATH (289)

Seven Mile Lane, Borough Green, Nr Sevenoaks, Kent

Tel: Borough Green 3072

Founded 1906 260 members

18 holes 5,801 yards S.S.S. 68 Sandy heath and parkland

Green fees Mon.-Fri. £1.65 per rd. £2.30 per day
Weekends with member only
Bona fide club members only

Professional H. Dearden

Membership Full subscription £25 p.a. (E.F. £35)

Visiting societies Max. 16 Terms by arrangement

Meals Bar snacks always available. Hot meals if ordered previous day

Nearest railway station Borough Green 3 miles

Hotels in vicinity White Rose, Wrotham Heath; Bull, Wrotham

WYKE GREEN (290)

Syon Lane, Isleworth, Middx. TW7 5PT

Tel: 01-560 8777

Founded 1928 500 members

18 holes 6,328 yards S.S.S. 70 Parkland

Green fees Mon.-Fri. £2.20 per rd./day
Weekends £3.30 per rd./day
Bona fide club members only

Professional G. Stoneman

Membership Full subscription £48 p.a. (E.F. £48)

Visiting societies Max. 40 Weekdays only. £4.50 per head

Meals Lunch and tea every day (except Tues.)

Nearest railway station Syon Lane ½ mile, Osterley (Piccadilly line tube) 1½ miles

Hotels in vicinity Europa Lodge, Hounslow